D0581692

Hertfordshire

522 667 30 6

J.J.
ABRAMS

# J.J. ABRAMS

## A STUDY IN GENIUS

NEIL DANIELS

JOHN BLAKE

Published by John Blake Publishing Ltd,
3 Bramber Court, 2 Bramber Road,
London W14 9PB, England

www.johnblakebooks.com

www.facebook.com/johnblakebooks
twitter.com/jblakebooks

This edition published in hardback in 2015

ISBN: 978 1 78418 775 0



British Library Cataloguing-in-Publication Data:

A catalogue record for this book is available from the British Library.

Design by www.envydesign.co.uk

Printed in Great Britain by CPI Group (UK) Ltd

1 3 5 7 9 10 8 6 4 2

## ABOUT THE AUTHOR

Neil Daniels is the author of numerous books on music and pop culture, including biographies of Metallica, AC/DC, Iron Maiden, Bon Jovi and Journey and John Blake titles on Matthew McConaughey and Martin Freeman. His books have been translated into over a dozen languages. His reviews, articles and interviews on music and pop culture have been published in *The Guardian*, *Record Collector*, *Rock Sound*, *Media Magazine* and *musicOMH*. He has also written several sets of sleeve notes for various record labels.

Neil lives in the North West of England. His official website is www.neildanielsbooks.com.

# CONTENTS

CHAPTER 1

# BEFORE HOLLYWOOD

'As a storyteller you have to love the characters…'

**J.J. Abrams, *The Daily Telegraph*, 2013**

It was almost inevitable that Jeffrey Jacob (J.J.) Abrams would enter the film industry given his family background: his father Gerald W. Abrams turned his hand to television producing after ending his career as a retail commercial contractor while his mother Carol Ann Abrams (maiden name Kelvin) was an executive producer after Abrams went to college (though she was actually a lawyer during J.J.'s youth) and his sister Tracy Rosen later became a screenwriter. It was the young J.J., however, who would one day take Hollywood by storm and become one of the most successful names in modern cinema.

Not since the peak of Steven Spielberg's commercial popularity in the 1980s had Hollywood produced a director of such obvious global appeal and cinematic charm. It was as if Abrams could do no wrong. He would one day relaunch not one, not two, but three major franchises and co-create one of the most talked-about TV shows of the 2000s. He would board the *Enterprise* and fly to a galaxy far, far away.

Is Abrams – the young-looking forty-nine-year-old with the curly dark hair, slightly geeky glasses and overall air of puppy-dog enthusiasm – a movie mogul? Indeed, is there any such thing as a movie mogul any more, in the mould of Sam Goldwyn, Lew Wasserman, Louis B. Mayer or Darryl Zanuck, men who simply ran the business back in the day? Well, in terms of personal success, there certainly is. George Lucas has a personal fortune of $5.4 billion, producer Arnon Milchan (*Pretty Woman*, *12 Years a Slave*) is second on the Hollywood rich list and scrapes by on $5.2 billion. Such men wield enormous influence. Abrams isn't in the top ten list yet – but of course personal wealth is not the only measure of moguldom. It is the sheer reach of Abrams's work on both the big and small screen that marks him out as a VIP mover and shaker. Albert (aka Cubby) Broccoli was a hard-working producer with over forty films under his belt: but only *one* world-conquering movie franchise, the Bond films? Alfred Hitchcock was a pretty good director but what do we find on the CV? Just the single solitary successful TV series? It can be argued that Abrams – as writer, producer and director – has already reached out to a bigger audience than both of them put together; he really is that big. He pulls off what is perhaps the most impressive filmic sleight-of-hand of them all (though some cineastes will disagree): he pleases all of the people some of the time – a feat accurately described by Anthony Lane in *The New Yorker*, who describes him as 'the perfect purveyor of fictions [that] will never jade.'

But what started it all? Abrams's first paid gig is almost

beyond belief. For a movie-obsessed kid, it must have been the equivalent of finding ET in the garage.

Jeffrey Jacobs Abrams was born in New York City on 27 June 1966, the same year an obscure science-fiction show called *Star Trek* was first broadcast, but eventually raised in the City of Angels where he attended Palisades High School.

Abrams was the typical nerd – obsessed with pop culture, especially movies and books. He could have been one of the Goonies. Abrams loved storytelling in all its manifestations. 'I remember being taught to read at a very early age,' he told *The New York Times* in late 2013. 'Like creepy young. I remember being in the crib, reading. My parents were very impressed. My reading speed, comprehension and overall ability has remained at that level ever since. There were always books around in the house, of course, and my parents did read to me sometimes, but my strongest memories of being read to are from kindergarten. Those teachers were excellent and made reading seem fun and adventurous.'

Abrams was drawn to the big screen over and above any other of his childhood hobbies and interests. Like anyone who aspires to become a film director, Abrams was drawn towards moving images. There was something about the way they tell a story that properly captured his attention. Abrams first picked up a camera aged eight and almost from the get-go his TV-producer father warned him against going into the notoriously unforgiving, not-to-say fickle, film industry. 'Making movies was more a reaction to not being chosen for sports,' Abrams said to *The Guardian*'s Steve Rose in 2009. 'Other kids were out there playing at whatever; I was off making something blow up and filming it, or making a mould of my sister's head using alginate plaster. So the answer is: yes, I was and am a geek.'

And Abrams also appreciated music and would one day become an amateur musician (and non-amateur composer). Was there any end to his talents? There were certain films Abrams adored while growing up, which gave him an appreciation for movie soundtracks. '*Jaws* was an incredible soundtrack,' he once told *Empire* film magazine. 'It had such a primal quality to it, but the sequence when all the boats go out like a regatta has this incredible seafaring note to it. John Williams did so much incredible stuff, his score to *The Fury* for Brian De Palma stands out, but *Jaws* was something else. I remember listening to it as a nine-year-old and finding it as scary and as intense as anything.'

Aged eleven and obsessed with films, J.J. Abrams first saw *Star Wars*. It blew his mind. *Star Wars* became the highest grossing film of all time after its 1977 release, even surpassing *Jaws*, which attacked an unsuspecting public in 1975 and is generally thought to have initiated the summer blockbuster season. Abrams adored the casting, the story, and the designs and just like any other kid his age who saw the film, he was transported by the space battles and all the action and adventure of the basic, good-versus-evil plot. Characters Darth Vader, Luke Skywalker, Princess Leia and Han Solo (and not forgetting the Droids R2-D2 and C-3PO) instantly became familiar names to anyone and everyone.

Abrams, like many other film buffs, not only took note of the directors but also the cast and crew of every film he watched. At the cinema, he stayed to the very end of every film to watch all the credits, when most of the audience had got up off their seats and left the auditorium.

One childhood friend of Abrams was Greg Grunberg, who later starred in some of Abrams's earliest TV productions including *Alias* and *Lost*. They made a childhood movie together called *The Attic* using a Super 8 camera. 'He shot it, then scratched in the monster, frame by frame. It was a bolt-of-lightning creature. He compensated ahead of time for where the monster would be,' Grunberg said to *USA Today*'s Bill Keveney in 2005. 'We were, like, eleven.'

Abrams's dad had an office at Paramount and when he was in his early teens J.J. would go with his dad to the office and hang out on the movie lot. The young Abrams got to know the security guards on the lot and they'd let him in on some of the sets to watch *Happy Days*, *Laverne And Shirley*, or *Mork And Mindy* starring a young Robin Williams. He got to see Mr Williams rehearsing his lines for *Mork And Mindy* and he remembers Ron Howard, later an acclaimed film director himself of course, and Henry Winkler from *Happy Days*. Abrams found the whole experience utterly fascinating and also a lot of fun. The best part was watching his dad, though. He'd visit sets with his dad and see how production worked and ask questions about this and that. He had been making Super 8 films since he was eight years old, so to see how TV shows were made was a dream come true. It fuelled his imagination and ambition. It drove his creativity. However, years later Abrams understood that as soon as you see how the finished product is made on set, the experience of watching a movie is changed.

He was especially a fan of the make-up artists and special

effects people. He loved the pre-computer-generated imagery such special effects wizards as John Dykstra, Dick Smith and Douglas Trumbull created, and adored the likes of Tom Savini and Stan Winston, whose creations looked as real as anything a computer could generate in the twenty-first century. 'I was definitely the fat kid making movies. I was the loner oddball kid who didn't have the confidence,' said Abrams to Jessica Furseth of *Idol Mag*. The fat kid making movies would later be recreated in Abrams's Spielbergian blockbuster, *Super 8*.

Abrams, much like his heroes Steven Spielberg – who'd begun making 8mm movies aged twelve in order to get a Boy Scout photography merit badge – and *The Twilight Zone* creator Rod Serling, was fascinated by moving pictures and how a sequence of images could tell a story with or without sound. Abrams, akin to almost all filmmakers, amateur or professional, strove to make the unreal seem real, and so he set himself movie-making assignments.

What's more, Abrams had a knack for storytelling, a flair for visuals. His grandfather used to take him to Tannen's Magic in New York City: one of the oldest magic stores in America. He quickly learned how to tell a story using images. The first magic trick he learned was with an egg cup – he loved learning how the egg disappeared. Magic is why he loves the movies and special effects – the ability to transform things and people or simply make them disappear. Special effects are really just an extension of old-school magic tricks.

'When I was a little kid – and even still – I loved magic tricks,' he later told *The Guardian*'s Katie Puckrik. 'When I saw how movies got made – at least had a glimpse when I went on the Universal Studios tour with my grandfather – I remember feeling like this was another means by which I could do magic. It wasn't the guy with the top hat and the rabbits, it was a way of creating illusions that something was real that wasn't. It could be a time and a place, it could be a weather system, it could be an aeroplane flying through the air, it could be a creature that wasn't really there, a fight scene, blood splattering, window breaking, fire – it could be anything. All these things were little magic tricks, and the idea that they could all add up to create the illusion that something was real, so that people would have an emotional reaction to the relationship, a circumstance, an event – that was very exciting to me.'

Abrams wasn't only interested in movies – he loved comic books and horror paperbacks too: '…for me what I remember so clearly and I think I was fourteen when *Night Shift*, the Stephen King short story collection came out,' he told CNN's Christian DuChateau. 'That blew my mind and I got obsessed with him and read *The Dead Zone* and *The Shining* and others. *Night Shift* did for me what *The Twilight Zone* did as a TV series.' Abrams would hook up with his literary hero in 2015 for a nine-hour mini-series based on King's time-travelling JFK related bestseller 11/22/63, starring James Franco.

Aged fifteen and fuelled by a fierce imagination and creative drive, Abrams came in contact with one of his heroes: none other than Mr Steven Spielberg, who was riding high after the success of the first *Indiana Jones* film, *Raiders of the Lost Ark* in 1981. Spielberg, who was always on the lookout for new talent, had read about Abrams and his Super 8 movie *High Voltage* in an *LA Times* profile titled *The Beardless Wonders of Filmmaking* after Abrams's Super 8 movie had been shown at the LA Film Festival. 'The Best Teen Super 8mm Films of

'81' ran at LA's Nuart Theatre in March 1982. The 'beardless' part of the title was a reference to the fact that many of the American filmmakers of the time – Spielberg, George Lucas, Martin Scorsese, Brian De Palma and Francis Ford Coppola – had beards.

A box of Spielberg's old Super 8 movies had been found by the person who moved into the house Spielberg grew up in in Arizona. The guy who found the box flipped open the lid and found the label 'Steven Spielberg'. The films were in disrepair and when they were returned to Spielberg he decided to restore them. Upon reading the article Spielberg thought Abrams and Reeves would be the right people for the job because they knew enough about Super 8 movies to carry out the task.

Spielberg's office called Abrams about the restoration project and offered $300 for the work. The call from Spielberg's office to Abrams was made by Kathleen Kennedy. Abrams elaborated to Jessica Furseth of *Idol Mag*: 'We were asked, "Would you be interested in repairing Spielberg's old 8mm films?" We were confused as hell by this. It made no sense at all. When I talk about this with him now he says, "Well I knew you guys would take care of it." I still don't believe him. It's a ridiculous story, but it's true.'

Abrams's partner on the restoration project was Matt Reeves, who went on to co-create the TV show *Felicity* with Abrams and direct *Cloverfield*, which Abrams produced. Reeves was at the festival with his twenty-eight-minute Hitchcock-inspired film *Stiletto*. They ended up cleaning Spielberg's films and re-splicing them. Were they dreaming? Was it a fantasy? It could not possibly have happened, but it did.

Spielberg would tell stories about the horror on his mother

Carol's face after seeing a pile of unspooled film rolls on the floor of her bedroom like spilled spaghetti. It was Abrams who many years later helped finish the job and make those 8mm rolls into watchable films. One of the films was *Firelight*, which was the precursor to the now iconic science-fiction tale *Close Encounters of the Third Kind*.

'...To this day it makes no sense to me why Steven would put the original prints of *Firelight* and *Escape to Nowhere* in the hands of two fifteen-year-old strangers,' Abrams told Richard Corliss of *Time Entertainment*. 'I mean, have you ever seen fifteen-year-olds? Don't give them things if you want them back. Especially repaired. But Matt and I did it. In 1982 it was especially rare, if not impossible, to have access to the early works of a director, let alone Steven Spielberg's. But while his films were, of course, far better than ours, it was an inspiration to see how he began.'

Also at the festival was Larry Fong (future cinematographer for *Lost* and *Super 8*) with the fifteen-minute spoof *Toast Encounters of the Burnt Kind*. Producers Bryan Burk and Lawrence Trilling were in attendance at the festival as well. It was the brainchild of Gerard Ravel, who hosted the public access show *Word of Mouth*, which was sort of the YouTube of its day. It was a thirty-minute interview format where talented (and some maybe not so talented) people could show their films. Anybody could put their own show out on public access. There was a cable system called Theta, which Z Channel was part of and they also had a public access channel called Channel 3. It was the golden age of public access TV where anybody could get an hour of broadcast time and put on his or her own show or film.

Ravel had offered assistance to Abrams with his *High Voltage* film by helping with the lighting, running him around various locations because he was only fifteen years old. There were some car chases in the film. Dom Deluise's oldest son Peter, an actor who later appeared in the TV series *21 Jump Street* opposite Johnny Depp, was one of Abrams's buddies who starred in *High Voltage*. Basically, Ravel produced while Abrams wrote and directed the film.

Ravel spoke to Todd Longwell of *Filmmaker Magazine* about the festival: 'At the end of our show, I'd say, "If you know anyone or you'd like to come on, here's our phone number. Give us a call." One day, I get a message on my phone machine. It said, "My name is J.J. I'm fifteen years old. I've been making films for seven years, and I would like to be on your show." I thought it was a prank...because most of my audience was older. So I called the number and I went over to his home [in LA's Pacific Palisades neighbourhood] and met him and his parents. They were really nice people and J.J. was one of the most polite, courteous kids I ever met. He loved working with makeup and special effects. He put the films on his Super 8 projector, and I knew this kid was going to make it. His enthusiasm was over the top, and as soon as I saw him, I said, "You know what? He's going to be a great interview. He's going to inspire other people to call my show." We ended up doing two shows [with Abrams]. Then the next week I get another call, and it's Matt Reeves. He says, "I'm fifteen years old. I saw J.J.'s films on your show. I have a thirty-minute film and I'd like to be on your show." That's when I knew I'd struck a chord, because now all of these kids who were wanting to be filmmakers were watching my show.'

Abrams and Reeves were integral to the creation of the

festival, after coming up with the idea with Ravel in October 1981. Reeves had introduced Bryan Burk to Abrams and they became best friends. Ravel had ninety minutes of new short films and booked a matinee at the cinema with just Abrams and Reeves onboard. They charged $3.50 per ticket. Even from this early age Abrams was something of a mini-movie mogul and a visionary. Creative Artists Agency people attended the festival and with the article in the *LA Times*, word was buzzing around Hollywood about these young filmmakers.

'…We'd all had the exact same experience of making these movies as kids,' Abrams said to *Time Out* Japan's David Fear. 'You know, trying to get your friends to take things seriously, when it's really like, "Jump out from behind that tree!" The ambitions are beyond the means at that point. When most kids were out playing sports in their yards, I was making these stupid little films with a home movie camera.'

Abrams took the restoration project as a fantastic opportunity to learn the craft of filmmaking. He got to see the earlier efforts of the man who directed such classic as *Jaws*, *Close Encounters of the Third Kind*, *E.T.* and *Raiders of the Lost Ark*. Sadly, Abrams never got the opportunity to meet his childhood director hero at the time but Spielberg did keep an eye on Abrams's career and the two directors finally met in person decades later.

Super 8 cameras gave budding filmmakers such as J.J. Abrams masterclasses in how to make small movies with limited resources. It was all about problem solving and how to extend your imagination to get the best results possible. Abrams spent much of his summer vacations making amateur movies and solving problems – how to make car crashes look real, how to make spaceships seem authentic and so on. The limited resources were problems that ultimately honed their storytelling skills.

Abrams spoke to Andrew Collins of the *Radio Times* years later about his career: 'The reason I even got into movies is because I wasn't the most popular kid: I wasn't into sports, I wasn't in the library studying all the time, I wasn't the kid playing chess or *Dungeons & Dragons* – I was in no group. And when I was eight and went to Universal Studios and saw how animation is done, make-up, special effects, it was immediately clear that this was the best thing in the world. I suddenly had a clear path.'

Whereas Reeves was afraid of horror films, Abrams loved them and when they'd have movie nights at each other's houses Abrams would want to watch horror. Along with Burk, Fong and others, they were movie buffs and budding filmmakers in much the same way baby boomers Spielberg, Lucas and Coppola and their peers were labelled the 'Movie Brats' in the 1970s. They would go on to follow their own individual paths but would all meet up in the long run. Abrams himself was not only a filmmaker but a writer and it was his talent as a wordsmith that would one day break him into Hollywood.

CHAPTER 2

# BREAKING INTO THE INDUSTRY

'In fairness, I don't think I've stopped writing dodgy screenplays...'

**J.J. Abrams, *Metro*, 2013**

Abrams's first Hollywood gig happened when he was sixteen years old and still an English student at Sarah Lawrence College on the East Coast. He was offered the job of writing the music for cult director Don Dohler's film, *Nightbeast*.

'…We would only see each other like over the summers,' producer Bryan Burk told *Collider*'s Steve 'Frosty' Weintraub about the friendship between himself, Abrams and Matt Reeves, which was much like that of George Lucas, Steven Spielberg and Robert Zemeckis in the 1980s, 'and really only started getting to be better friends after college when he was done. But suffice it to say, we'd always been friends.'

Released in 1982, the very same year *E.T.* was released and became the highest-grossing film of all time, even surpassing *Star Wars*. *Nightbeast* is a loose follow-up to Dohler's debut film *The Alien Factor* and concerns a small-town sheriff who attempts to prevent an alien from killing the residents of the little settlement of Perry Hall. The film features much the same cast as *The Alien Factor*. The production is noted for the opening credit sequence by the greatly revered Ernest Farino, who created the opening title effects for *The Terminator*, *The Abyss* and *Terminator 2: Judgement Day*; all directed by the Canadian-born filmmaker James Cameron, one of the most successful filmmakers in Hollywood and a special effects pioneer and noted science-fiction enthusiast. The alien itself was created by John Dods; later known for his work on *Ghostbusters 2*, *Alien Resurrection* and *The X-Files*. No doubt to capitalise on Abrams's growing success, *Nightbeast* was released on DVD in early 2009.

Abrams spoke to *Metro*'s Andrew Williams in 2013 about his experiences writing screenplays at college: 'In fairness, I don't think I've stopped writing dodgy screenplays. When I was in college I wrote around ten screenplays. Some were about young people going through crazy adventures. Some were more offbeat – there was always an odd love story at the core of it. It was the beginning of wanting to try to figure out how to write a screenplay. There's never a moment you go from being an amateur writer doing the best you can to being a professional writer who does great – you're always doing the same thing but if you're lucky at some point, you make a living from it. I don't feel any different when I sit down to write something today than I did back in college. It still starts with: "What if I did this?"'

Working on low-budget schlock films is often the best way to gain experience, usually the only way. Abrams – like his peers in the industry – was inspired by the directors and producers of the late 1960s and 1970s in an era of New Hollywood after the demise of the studio system, when studios had actors and directors under contract and could dictate which films they could and could not make. The studio system was almost Orwellian in its dictatorship.

With the studio system broken and the ground-breaking French New Wave still in mind, which brought unconventional forms of storytelling to cinema by such filmmaking intellects as Jean Luc Godard and Francois Truffaut, a generation of American film students – baby boomers born in the 1940s and raised in the prosperous 1950s, coming out of the suburbs of California, or from small-town America or the tough streets of New York – broke new ground with often violent and unconventional films such as *Bonnie and Clyde* and *Easy Rider* and later the two *Godfather* films and *Taxi Driver*. Directors such as Francis Ford Coppola, Brian De Palma and Martin Scorsese worked on low-budget B exploitation movies for Roger Corman, which gave them the experience and knowledge they needed to make their own films. They were not only film students who studied the history and theory of cinema but they were also film fanatics who knew European cinema as much as American cinema.

However, while the likes of Scorsese and De Palma refused to be censored and conform to box-office needs, George Lucas and Steven Spielberg came from a different school of thought with influences that ranged from comic books to sci-fi movies and the suburban American culture of their youth, as shown in Lucas's classic *American Graffiti*. Before Lucas hit gold with *Star Wars* in 1977, his first movie was an interesting low-budget dystopian science-fiction tale call *THX-1138,* but it didn't attract the kind of audience that *Star Wars* would! Abrams would take what he'd learned from those people, Spielberg and Lucas especially, and build a career in Hollywood that was unparalleled within his generation of filmmakers.

After *Nightbeast* the jobs slowly rolled in. He wrote a film treatment with Jill Mazursky during his senior year in college, which was picked up by Touchstone Pictures and was used as the basis for the movie *Taking Care of Business*. This was Abrams's first produced film and stars Charles Grodin and James Belushi. Directed by Arthur Hiller, who was behind such films as *Author! Author!*, *The Lonely Guy* and *See No Evil, Hear No Evil*, *Taking Care of Business* is a comedy about a hot-headed advertising executive whose entire life is noted in a Filofax organiser that ends up in the hands of an affable convict, who uses it for his own ends to pose as the ad man. It received negative reviews upon its 1990 release and only grossed $20 million at the box office.

Caryn James wrote of the film in *The New York Times*: 'Mr. Belushi is the film's one good feature. He makes Jimmy a likable boor, just smart enough to pull off this hoax. When he wins the tennis game by swinging the racquet like a baseball bat, he suggests the kind of loopy humour that *Taking Care of Business* seldom approaches. But everyone else seems to have phoned in the film, including Mr. Grodin at his whiniest and Arthur Hiller, the veteran director of films as funny as *The In-Laws* and as unspeakable as *Love Story*. *Taking Care of Business* plays it safe and boring.'

Following *Taking Care of Business*, Abrams wrote the touching drama *Regarding Henry* starring Harrison Ford and Annette Bening, released in 1991. Directed by the much respected

Mike Nichols, known for the films *The Graduate*, *Working Girl* and *Postcards from the Edge*, *Regarding Henry* is about a New York City lawyer who faces an uphill battle trying to regain his memory, mobility and speech after a shooting in a convenience store robbery. Abrams also had a small part in the film as the Delivery Boy.

Barry McIlheney wrote of the film in *Empire*: '*Regarding Henry* is ultimately just about bearable thanks to Ford's sheer presence and the occasional reminder, the first twenty minutes in particular, of what might and should have been.'

Resident *Rolling Stone* film critic Peter Travers wrote: 'Given the reputations of star Harrison Ford and director Mike Nichols, one expects more from their first collaboration since *Working Girl* than this slick tearjerker. The script, by twenty-four-year-old Jeffrey Abrams (*Taking Care of Business*), has a knack for trivializing the big issues it strenuously raises.'

At this point Abrams was not following any clear career plan other than to get as much work as possible. It's interesting to see how different his earlier scripts are from his later productions. His TV and movie interests were eclectic. 'Growing up, I loved *The Twilight Zone* as much as I loved *The Mary Tyler Moore Show*,' he confessed to *The A.V. Club*'s Noel Murray. 'And I loved the *Superman* TV show when I was a kid, and *Batman*, and *Speed Racer*, and all the pop-culture icons that everyone in my generation lived on. But I also remember loving the version of *The Hunchback of Notre Dame* with Charles Laughton. I watched it when I was ten or eleven, and was just sobbing over the story, while also being blown away by the makeup. My favourite things have nearly always been extreme and fantastical, involving some kind of visual effects, but also very emotionally driven. I loved *Ordinary People*, and *The Philadelphia Story*, and a lot of dramas and comedies based on plays that could not be farther from science-fiction. And at the same time, I was obsessed with the horror movies of the early eighties and late seventies. So in the end, the things I've worked on professionally have really been whatever I've been lucky enough to get produced, not stuff that I planned out years in advance.'

Abrams continued to write more scripts and sell them to Hollywood producers. His next scripted film, which he also executive produced, was a more or less forgotten gem called *Forever Young*. The script sold for a staggering $2 million. It was released in 1992 and stars Mel Gibson as a 1939 test pilot named Daniel McCormick who asks his best friend to cryogenically freeze him for a year so that he does not watch the love of his life die. Doctors have told him she will probably never recover from the coma that she is in after an accident. McCormick does not wake up a year later, but in 1992. The film received mixed reviews but fared reasonably well at the box office. Mel Gibson was one of Hollywood's biggest stars by the early 1990s with the *Lethal Weapon* and *Mad Max* films to his name. The film also starred a young Elijah Wood, best known these days as Frodo Baggins in *Lord of the Rings*, and Jamie Lee Curtis as his on-screen mother.

Writing in *The New York Times*, Vincent Canby said of the film: '*Forever Young* looks to be very much a star vehicle. Because of that, it may not be fair to blame either the writer or director for its lack of narrative focus. The star is the centre of everything. The physical production is handsome and elaborate, but nothing deflects attention from Mr. Gibson for any length of time, not even Ms. Curtis. Ms. Glasser is not around long enough to establish her own screen presence. Even George Wendt, the formidably funny *Cheers* star, who plays the inventor of Daniel's deep-freeze chamber, does not make much of an impression.'

The 1990s were flying by for Abrams as he was picking up as much work as possible and gaining invaluable experience in the industry. Abrams spent much of the decade working on scripts and selling them to studios. He was waiting for his big break and while it takes a long time for some (less so for others, while for many it never happens) it gave him a chance to refine his craft and hone his scriptwriting skills.

In 1993 Abrams had a small part as the character Doug in *Six Degrees of Separation*, based on the Pulitzer-Prize-nominated play by John Guare. The film was a critical success and won Stockard Channing Oscar and Golden Globe nominations for Best Actress. Abrams wasn't the first and neither would he be the last writer-producer-director (though not a director at this point) to venture in front of the camera. Scorsese has had small acting parts; Quentin Tarantino has had leading roles and Hitchcock most famously had cameos in most of his motion pictures.

He scripted (with Jill Mazursky) the 1993 comedy *Gone Fishin'* which stars Joe Pesci and Danny Glover, who had previously appeared on screen together in the successful buddy-cop movies *Lethal Weapon 2* and *Lethal Weapon 3*. Directed by Christopher Cain, *Gone Fishin'* sees Pesci and Glover star as two bumbling fishing fanatics who get into trouble after their boat gets stolen on a fishing trip. It was released by Hollywood

Films, a brand of Walt Disney. The film pretty much sank without a trace.

Writing in *The New York Times*, Lawrence Van Gelder said: 'With Joe Pesci and Danny Glover as bait, Hollywood Pictures is trolling for dollars aboard a new comedy called *Gone Fishin'*. It's a sinker. This is a film that misses the boat right from the start through an improper mixture of fools. Effervescent comic chemistry normally bubbles out of the pairing of volatile opposites, typically a sensible straight man and a blithering idiot à la Laurel and Hardy, Abbott and Costello and Martin and Lewis.'

Another film Abrams worked on as a scriptwriter was 1995's *Casper* produced by Amblin Entertainment and written by Sherri Stoner and Deanna Oliver. 'At this time in his career, [Abrams] wasn't yet a director, but a writer, and he was a great writer,' recalled Amblin Entertainment co-founder Steven Spielberg to *Entertainment Weekly*. 'He was very witty and he adores plot structure and storytelling. There are a lot of writers who write brilliant dialogue and who can do wonderful confrontational drama and comedy. But not everybody knows story. Whether it's a character story or a pure plot-driven story, J.J. is amazing.' The CGI-pioneering *Casper* was an international success.

Abrams had also been invited by Amblin to pitch ideas for a sequel to the live action animation classic *Who Framed Roger Rabbit?* directed by Robert Zemeckis. Abrams didn't get the job and neither was a sequel made.

Never one to stay idle, and continuing to work his way around various Hollywood projects, Abrams then produced the 1996 film *The Pallbearer* under the moniker of Jeffrey Abrams. The film stars David Schwimmer, Gwyneth Paltrow and Toni

Collette and follows the trials of a young man whose life becomes rather complicated when he is asked to be a pallbearer at the funeral of a former classmate he does not even recall. He also reacquaints himself with an old high school crush after she temporarily revisits her home town. The romantic comedy hardly won over audiences or critics, though it does have its fans. Kind of.

*Chicago Sun-Times*'s Roger Ebert was circumspect. 'To begin with the obvious: *The Pallbearer* is a goofier, gloomier trek across some of the same ground covered in *The Graduate*, with David Schwimmer of TV's *Friends* in the Dustin Hoffman role. The filmmakers must have subjected the 1967 classic to minute scrutiny. And yet the movie is not simply a retread; it has its own originality and tone and a quirkier sense of humour, and the central role is ideal for Schwimmer's hangdog charm.'

'It doesn't take long to see that the folks who made *The Pallbearer*, screenwriter Jason Katims and his co-writer and director, Matt Reeves, have cribbed rather shamelessly from *The Graduate*,' Owen Gleiberman wrote in *Entertainment Weekly*. 'What's more, they've done it without devising any equivalent to the glib yet satisfying sociocultural whimsy ("Plastics") that gave that movie its zeitgeist cachet. *The Pallbearer* is *The Graduate* Lite, a romantic-mix-up comedy that taps all too modestly into the awkward emotional tribulations of being twenty-five years old.'

Abrams's PR executive wife told him that it was important to work on projects that meant something to him personally, though he did have to make creative sacrifices, but such is the nature of the job. 'I was part of that machine of screenwriters that goes from project to project,' he explained to *The Guardian*'s

Andrew Pulver, 'but over the years had found myself doing things that weren't so meaningful.'

As the 1990s was drawing to a close those meaningful projects were getting close.

CHAPTER 3

# MOVE TO THE SMALL SCREEN

'Movies were always – for me as a kid – the thing.'

**J.J. Abrams, BBC, 2013**

Abrams's biggest success to date arrived in 1998 with the science-fiction blockbuster *Armageddon*, which he scripted with five other writers in the long and convoluted scriptwriting process that is typical of Hollywood. It stars Bruce Willis and Ben Affleck and was directed by Michael Bay, who'd had blockbuster hits with the action flicks *Bad Boys* and *The Rock*. Though a major box office success, the film was panned by critics and was released after the Morgan Freeman-led asteroid-strike movie, *Deep Impact*. The basic premise of *Armageddon*, as ridiculous as it sounds, is that a group of working-class deep core drillers and engineers is hired by NASA to destroy a huge asteroid that is on a path to collide with Earth.

'How do I hate *Armageddon*?' exclaimed Peter Travers in his review of the film for *Rolling Stone*. 'Let me count the ways. I hate it to the depth and breadth and height of its greedy confidence that a jumbo promotion budget (reportedly a record $100 million) can herd an audience into anything – even a formulaic epic about an asteroid the size of Texas that's on a collision course with Earth. This despite the fact that a similar collection of space clichés was launched back in May, in *Deep Impact*.'

*Chicago Sun-Times*'s Roger Ebert wrote: 'Here it is at last, the first 150-minute trailer. *Armageddon* is cut together like its own highlights. Take almost any thirty seconds at random, and you'd have a TV ad. The movie is an assault on the eyes, the ears, the brain, common sense and the human desire to be entertained. No matter what they're charging to get in, it's worth more to get out.'

In the same vein Angie Errigo wrote in *Empire*: 'The latest entry in the "let's kick some asteroid butt" stakes is a doomsday countdown spectacle from producer Jerry Bruckheimer and "Bad Boy" Bay that extends their commitment to extreme tosh. With no messing about, this opens on the demolition of downtown Manhattan plus the imperilment of a nice little dog, all within a few minutes. Yikes! It's a meteor shower, heralding "the worst parts of the Bible" to come, and the first of a thousand-and-one big bangs: whenever there's a lull in proceedings, there's a wake-up call such as the splattering of Shanghai or – a highlight – the annihilation of Paris.'

*Armageddon* was nominated for a Razzie Award (opposite to the Oscars, honouring bad films) for Worst Screenplay. *Armageddon* now stands as one of the most memorable films of the decade but not necessarily for the right reasons. It was not the sort of film that Abrams wanted to make and little, if any, of it is reminiscent of his other work; but the film gave him experience in the world of Hollywood screenwriting. Abrams would continue to work on all sorts of TV series and Hollywood movies but his big break was yet to arrive.

*The Suburbans*, which Abrams produced, was released in 1999. The comedy stars *I Know What You Did Last Summer* and *Party of Five* actress Jennifer Love Hewitt and Donal Lardner Ward (who also wrote and directed the film) and satirises the revival of the 1980s toward the end of the century. The film was neither a commercial nor critical success.

'With fewer distractions and the slightest smidgen of wit,' wrote Doug Brod in *Entertainment Weekly*, 'the movie might have made an amusing companion to the terrific *Still Crazy*. But director, cowriter, and nominal star Donal Lardner Ward (*My Life's in Turnaround*) prefers to indulge in the kind of insipid relationship navel gazing and ludicrously overripe dialogue that's all the rage in vanity indie productions.'

The end of the 1990s was also the time when Abrams made his first foray into television with *Felicity*, which ran for four seasons on The WB Network. It ran against the likes of *Sex and the City*, *Charmed*, *Dawson's Creek*, *That '70s Show* and *Will And Grace* in the TV listings, but did not quite have such an enduring appeal as those shows.

A self-confessed genre buff all his life, and having just worked on *Armageddon*, Abrams suddenly found himself involved in something completely different. There were no outer space explosions. It was about college stuff like grade results and relationships.

'A TV show typically needs a door that every week bursts open with the burden that the main characters have to hold,'

Abrams explained to the *Nerdist*, 'carry and deal with, and help people in a selfless way. The model of a TV show is a condition that characters can actually deal with stuff that's not just their own issues, college is only about your own issues. I'm not saying we didn't do shootings at parties and dramatic breakups, and horrible stories. There were things that were substantial; whether it was anything from date-rape to drug use – there were all these kind of things that were where you need to go to find stories, and of course there are things that are sadly very relevant to that age, but typically it was [very difficult] to come up with what's the "thing" every week.'

He acted as the show's co-creator with Matt Reeves, who directed the pilot, and executive producer with Brian Grazer and Ron Howard (yes *that* Ron Howard of *Happy Days* fame) of Imagine Entertainment as the show's producers.

It ran for four seasons until 2002 and concerned the college life of its main character Felicity Porter, played by Keri Russell. Abrams wasn't entirely sure if Russell was right for the part at first because she was too attractive, with gorgeous hair and good looks, whereas Felicity has no friends. Russell, though, won him over in the audition. (She had been one of the golden generation cast of Disney's *All-New Mickey Mouse Club* alongside Ryan Gosling, Christina Aguilera, Britney Spears and Justin Timberlake.)

Felicity is from Palo Alto in California but attends the University of New York (based on New York University) and each season revolves around the traditional divisions of American college life from freshman year to sophomore, junior and senior years.

'...*Felicity* is really a character piece,' Reeves said to *Den of Geek*'s Sarah Dobbs, 'and it was very intimate and there's a lot of people in rooms talking to each other, relationship stuff, but the thing that was important to me – you know J.J. and I created that show together and I directed a number of episodes, I directed the pilot – was that we were always trying to go for a kind of naturalism. It was this college fantasy but there was a lot of naturalism with the actors and the situations we tried to create.'

It was in television where Abrams slowly started to make a name for himself but when it finally happened, it would happen with a big splash, and it would seem to many that he came out of nowhere.

A lot of viewers could relate to the show; she became a role model for a lot of people so Abrams and Reeves had to be careful with the storylines. They sort of had a moral obligation to be true to the character and her audience. They felt responsible to those teen viewers, which is often the case with any show aimed at a young audience. 'For *Felicity*,' Abrams said in 2000 to *Checkout.com*, 'we just want to make sure that she's taking risks, she's taking chances and if she does something stupid – like takes too many Jell-O shots at the frat party and ends up in a compromising situation – that there are real consequences to it. I also think it's not just *Felicity*. I mean, it's all the characters. For example, Donald Faison – who's in this new movie *Remember the Titans* and he's amazing – he plays Tracy, a virgin on the show and we have a storyline coming up where we really didn't want and don't want the impression that if you're a virgin, you lose your girlfriend. So how do we do a story where Elena possibly cheats on Tracy without it being that? You have to make it clear that the reason these things happen is not because she's not getting sex from him. It has to be about a bigger issue. So that kind of stuff is important for young men as well. For the six young men who watch.'

*Felicity* was a drama about real-life issues that concern young Americans at college. It was an intimate series with a lot of people talking in rooms about relationships and life choices.

'I miss writing for a show that doesn't have any sort of odd, almost sci-fi bend to it,' Abrams admitted to *The Hollywood Reporter*'s Lacey Rose years later. 'It was just sort of pure romantic, sweet characters who had crushes on one another and were dealing with which party to go to and if they had a part-time job or not – stuff that was kind of fun to write about.'

The show was a critical success and was ranked in *Time Magazine*'s 2007 poll of '100 Best TV Shows of All Time'. Michele Greppi wrote in the *New York Post*: '*Felicity* is not as flip as *Buffy the Vampire Slayer* and not as hip as *Dawson's Creek*. But it is more than 'Ally McBeal Goes to College' or 'My So-Called College Life'...It's an intelligent and gentle ode to the painful joys of growing up, one mistake at a time.'

On the other side of the coin Jonathan Storm wrote in *The Philadelphia Inquirer*: '*Felicity* is phony. It presents a fantasy world, pretending it's real. A lot of people criticize *Ally McBeal* for the same thing, but there's a big difference. The people in their twenties who would take life cues from Ally should be old enough to know better. The people, many not even teenagers yet, who will be learning from *Felicity* may not be...Actually, there are two big differences. *Ally McBeal* is entertaining.'

Clearly, the series is something very different from the latter-day science-fiction themes of Abrams's future TV work.

'...I must say how much I miss working on that show,'

Abrams admitted to *BuddyTV*'s Debbie Chang years later. 'It was such a wonderful group and a really fun time, and the cast was just awesome. And having never done it before, it was a whole new experience. It was surreal, it was hard, but it was also a very special group, so I miss them a lot.'

*Felicity* was a hit but his next TV show would be even bigger. Abrams went on to create and executive-produce the hit ABC TV show *Alias*, which ran from 2001 to 2006. The year it was launched it had stiff competition in the TV listings against *24*, *Smallville*, *Six Feet Under*, *Law And Order: Criminal Intent* and *Scrubs*.

The whole idea of *Alias* when Abrams pitched it to the network was, 'What if *Felicity* was a spy?' Abrams told the *Nerdist*: 'ABC/Touchstone came to me and said "we're looking to do a show that's a young, female-driven show, would you have something?" [I shared my idea with the head of the studio] about a young girl who's a spy and she's in Grad school, because I know you can't in Episode 16 say "and *Felicity*'s a spy" and they said "that sounds great why don't you write it," and so I put the *Run Lola Run* soundtrack on and I listened to it non-stop and wrote the *Alias* pilot to that score and I turned it in. They said "Who do you want to direct it?", and I heard myself say "me" and they said "OK" and I thought "they're crazy", and we cast the show with Jennifer Garner who had been on *Felicity*, so it was fun.'

Indeed, Garner had played a supporting role in *Felicity* since 1998 and it was Abrams who approached her for the role of Sydney Bristow. It would be a big step up for Garner, who was not used to roles involving high kicks, punches and action scenes. She had no background in martial arts or gymnastics so she enrolled in a private four-week Taekwondo class for the audition. She was finally cast after a few auditions. Even on her first day of shooting she was nervous about the action scenes, thinking she couldn't do them. Her stunt double, Shauna Duggins, helped her through the series.

Similarly to Joss Whedon, creator of *Buffy The Vampire Slayer*, Abrams, whether it is consciously expressed or not, is a feminist. Much of his work has strong female characters and as Whedon has noted in the past, strong female leads have often been lacking in science-fiction and fantasy films and TV. There's Ripley in the *Alien* movies, Sarah Connor in the *Terminator* films and spin-off TV series and of course, *Buffy*, but little else. Though *Alias* is not outright science-fiction it does have some sci-fi trappings, especially in the latter seasons.

Abrams was spending so much time in the writers' room during season one of *Alias* that he was obliged to sacrifice time working on the cuts. Usually, it's the directing producer who supervises the cuts for the show until the showrunner, the person who runs the show on a day-to-day basis, comes in and confirms the final shots. The directing producer for several of the first season's episodes was Ken Olden and because he was so busy prepping the scenes before he shot them, Abrams asked Bryan Burk to step in during the middle of season one. Burk didn't really have much enthusiasm for TV work but because Abrams was a friend and needed another helping hand, Burk agreed. Burk thought he'd be out after season one but he started talking ideas for season two to be aired in 2002 and then the idea of setting up a production company was brought up and, for Abrams and Burk, everything would change.

In 2001 Abrams founded the production company Bad Robot with Bryan Burk. It was initially part of Touchstone Television. Burk would become an integral part of Abrams's life and career.

Burk was born on 30 December 1968 and attended USC's School of Cinema-Television before breaking into the industry by working with producers Brad Weston at Columbia Pictures, John Davis at Fox and Ned Tanen at Sony. He moved over to Gerber Pictures in 1995 where he created *James Dean* for TNT, which was nominated for an Emmy. Working together under the Bad Robot umbrella, Abrams and Burk would create some of the most successful and popular TV shows and films of the 2000s and beyond.

Bad Robot would take Hollywood by storm. Of course Abrams's inspiration for the company was Amblin Entertainment, founded by Steven Spielberg in 1981, with producers Kathleen Kennedy and Frank Marshall. Amblin inspired a generation of filmmakers from Chris Columbus to Joe Dante and Robert Zemeckis. Remember those 'Steven Spielberg Presents' movies? Amblin was also responsible for some of the most successful films of the 1990s, including *The Goonies*, *Back to the Future*, *Gremlins*, *Who Framed Roger Rabbit?*, *Batteries not Included* and *Innerspace*. Most filmmakers who grew up in the 1980s were inspired by Amblin. It would have been hard not to be, such was the cultural impact of those films. They would start developing shows under the Bad Robot moniker and sign a TV deal with Warners and a film deal with Paramount.

'Bad Robot is very much a little ecosystem not unlike Pixar in that it's able to function with a big studio but able to have a measure of autonomy and freedom to go in quirky directions and do things a little off the beaten track,' future Abrams collaborator and *Mission: Impossible – Ghost Protocol* director Brad Bird said to *Indiewire*'s Drew Taylor.

*Alias* was a good enough show to kick-start Bad Robot; it was cool, sexy, action-packed and stylish. It had millions of loyal followers around the globe. The show, which ran for five years, saw Jennifer Garner in the role of a CIA agent named Sydney Bristow, who tries to keep her career as an agent for the government a secret from her family and friends, so she assumes various aliases to carry out her tasks.

'I love great characters wherever they come from,' Abrams said to one interviewer at *Salty Popcorn*, 'and I've always tried to write characters that just regardless of what their sex or race or background are, are compelling and interesting, and you know I've succeeded not as often as I'd like and you know, we try and you just keep doing what you can do and um, Sydney Bristow [the lead character in *Alias* played by Jennifer Garner] was not necessarily written as a strong female, she was just written as a strong character that happens to be a woman.'

Latter seasons saw heavy use of intricate technologies that made the show delve into science-fiction themes (the world's drinking water polluted with a drug for example, a machine that engenders insanity, and the search for immortality). It was a long-running hit and a firm cult classic for genre fans. It won over audiences and critics, and received various awards and nominations. *Alias* would prove to be one of Abrams's most enduring TV creations and a personal favourite. 'I suppose my favourite that I've created was Sydney Bristow, the central character from the TV series *Alias*,' he told *The New York Times* in 2013. 'She was a character with a secret, and that is always a fun place to start. I love how she was sweet and romantic and looked like the girl next door, but was also lethal and brave as hell, and would do nearly anything for love of country. But she wasn't a superhero; she was terrified at almost every step. But still, she would do the right thing. I think we would all like to believe we would behave like that when the going gets tough.'

*Alias* was a critical and commercial hit from the get-go. It opened to around 10 million viewers per episode for the first half of season one, and such was the success of the series that Garner's salary ran from $40,000 an episode to $150,000 by the end of the first series. Garner won an award for 'Best Actress in a Television Series – Drama' at the 2002 Golden Globe Awards. She later won further awards and nominations for her role.

Ken Tucker wrote of *Alias* in *Entertainment Weekly*: 'The whole show is complicated in a fun, brain-teasing way, and having seen the second episode, I can say it only gets funner. I know that's not a word, but I'm saying it anyway.'

And David Bianculli wrote in the *New York Daily News*: '*Alias* is so captivating because the actors and the writers make you believe in the characters, the situations and the jeopardy. There's a lot of humour, too, in both the romantic relationship and the James Bond-style spy gadgetry. And there are plenty of surprising turns.'

The TV series made a star of lead actress Jennifer Garner who took time out to star in the pretty dire 2005 Marvel superhero movie *Elektra*. 'It's J.J.,' Garner said to *USA Today*'s Bill Keveney about returning to the show. 'He has helped make *Alias* a family for me. I'd keep coming back for him as long as he wants and (as long as) there's an audience for the show.'

Garner even directed an episode of the fourth season called 'In Dreams'. 'I loved it,' she told *Moviefone*'s Jessie Heyman of her experience as a director. 'I had so much fun because my crew wanted me to do it and they really made it great for me. [But] it's too much of a time commitment. I can't imagine. A house can only hold one director, as far as I can tell.'

After five seasons of *Alias*, Abrams knew it had reached its natural conclusion. They got the chance to tie everything up, which is not something that happens all that often in TV shows. It was nevertheless a bittersweet moment for all concerned, especially Abrams, who adored the cast and crew. It was a good, satisfying end to a fantastic series. Garner became an executive producer on the final season, which finished in May 2006. It was shortened to seventeen episodes from twenty-two, owing to Garner's pregnancy with husband Ben Affleck, whom she met during the making of *Daredevil.* The pregnancy was written into the storyline. Garner would go on to star in a host of Hollywood films and independents including *The Kingdom*, *Juno*, *Ghosts of Girlfriends Past*, *Arthur* and *The Off Life of Timothy Green*. She remains best known for *Alias* and *Elektra*.

Asked at the 2006 WonderCon if there was a possibility of an *Alias* film, which is an idea fans would love to see become a reality, Abrams said: 'I think at the moment, right now *Alias* is sort of going to rest in just the right way, so I think that it's the right way for it to go out.'

Garner, however, expressed interest in going back to *Alias* for a movie; but only if Abrams and the rest of the cast and crew were involved. It seems unlikely at this stage, though. Garner even admitted that she'd never seen a full series all the way through; just random episodes. 'One night I ran across an episode of *Alias* and it was the weirdest thing,' Garner told *Moviefone*'s Jessie Heyman. 'A lot of episodes maybe I saw but I was so busy at the time, I don't think I even saw them all. Someday I want to go back and watch them. I felt like I was watching a different person. I didn't know what I was talking about, I kind of remembered the outfit but I started speaking another language that I didn't remember learning and then I did a fight I didn't remember. It was crazy.'

It was during the five seasons of *Alias* that Abrams would meet some of his longest-running collaborators. One of the producers and writers of the show (from 2001 to 2003) was Alex Kurtzman who would become a frequent collaborator with Abrams. Kurtzman was born on 7 September 1973 and raised in Los Angeles. He met fellow aspiring writer and future collaborator Roberto Orci at the private high school, Crossroads, in Santa Monica when they were both seventeen. Kurtzman then attended Wesleyan University while Orci went to The University of Texas in Austin. The pair first began writing together on the TV show *Hercules: The Legendary Journeys*. Aged twenty-four, they were placed in charge of the show after actor Kevin Sorbo suffered a stroke. Kurtzman and Orci created several storylines together during Sorbo's absence. Before hooking up with Abrams on *Alias* the pair also worked on *Xena: Warrior Princess* and *Jack of All Trades*.

Roberto Gaston Orci was born on 20 July 1973 in Mexico City to a Cuban mother and Mexican father and raised in Texas and LA. His mother had immigrated with her parents after the rise of Fidel Castro's communist government. Orci's older brother, J.R., is also a screenwriter-producer.

*Alias,* in addition, led Abrams to meet another one of his future collaborators, composer Michael Giacchino. Michael Giacchino was born on 10 October 1967 in Riverside, New Jersey. He was hired by Universal after doing an unpaid internship while studying for a degree at the School of Visual Arts in NYC. He graduated in 1990 and attended music classes at the prestigious Juilliard School. He subsequently worked at Disney after they relocated to Los Angeles and took night classes in instrumentation and orchestration at UCLA. After making contacts at Disney he eventually started composing music for video games at Disney Interactive before branching out and working with DreamWorks and Pandemic studios. He composed the music for such popular games as the *Medal of Honour* and *Call of Duty* games. It was through his video games that Abrams discovered Giacchino and chose him to compose the music for *Alias*.

Throughout the noughties, despite his move into TV, Abrams continued to work on films and co-wrote and produced the thriller *Joy Ride* in 2001, a work undoubtedly inspired by Steven Spielberg's 1971 feature debut *Duel*. From a script by acclaimed author Richard Matheson, adapted from his own short story and starring Dennis Weaver, *Joy Ride* was renamed *Roadkill* in some countries and directed by John Dahl, the director of the neo-noir classics *Red Rock West* and *The Last Seduction* in the early 1990s. *Joy Ride* stars the late Paul Walker, Steve Zahn and Leelee Sobieski and follows the story of three young people on a road trip to New Jersey from Colorado. They try to escape from a trucker they'd been talking to on their CB radio after he turns out to be a psychotic killer. The film was a reasonable success at the box office and received mostly positive reviews from film critics.

Jo'C wrote in *Time Out*: 'Dahl's surprisingly effective mad trucker thriller, his most enjoyable offering since *The Last Seduction*, is a mesh of quotations from classics like *Duel* and *The Hitcher*.'

Ed Gonzalez said of the film in *Slant Magazine*: 'Typically efficient for a Dahl film, *Joy Ride* still smells of Hollywood. Mr. Rusty forces Lewis and Fuller to walk naked into a diner during the film's best scene. This attention to sexual humiliation, though, is entirely too softcore. Has Mr. Rusty even seen *Deliverance*? Dahl does the best he can with cornfields, motel rooms and a few music oldies but *Joy Ride* is entirely too noisy to ever deserve a place next to Spielberg's *Duel*.'

A year later Abrams wrote a script for a fifth *Superman* film that is unlikely ever to be produced. 'I wrote a script for a *Superman* years ago,' he said to one interviewer at *Salty Popcorn*, 'that ended up being reviewed online and it was, you know, a work in progress, it was not a completed script and I was just decimated, the reaction…it was a very interesting thing because it was one of those things that…it happened in a way that on the one hand I was like horrified and on the other hand it was very educational; and I realise when people hold something near and dear to their heart there are certain things you don't mess with.'

Bad Robot's biggest success to date, however, was just around the corner.

CHAPTER 4

# LOST ON AN ISLAND

'I believe in anything that will engage the audience
and make the story more effective.'
**J.J. Abrams, *Time*, 2011**

Abrams's biggest success arrived in 2004 with the cult television series *Lost*, which he co-created and executive-produced with Damon Lindelof and Jeffrey Lieber. Lindelof would become a key figure at Bad Robot; he had originally met Abrams in 2004 when he pitched for a job on *Alias* but it was *Lost* that brought the pair together.

Born Damon Laurence Lindelof on 24 April 1973 in New Jersey, he cut his teeth in television in the 1990s with *Crossing Jordan* and *Nash Bridges*. He attended film school in New York before moving to LA after graduating. Much of his work, especially *Lost*, contains many references to novelist Stephen King, who is one of Lindelof's heroes. Another influence was the seminal graphic novel *Watchmen* by the renowned Alan Moore. The show averaged 15.6 million viewers during its first year and, though ratings subsequently dipped, it retained a core fan base.

'[*Lost*] was very much about faith versus science, and the notion of who has had a profound impact on your life and how these characters form a kind of tapestry,' Abrams explained to *The Guardian*'s Katie Puckrik. 'When you do a show that has that kind of ongoing conversation, the audience not only invests in the show in ways that you could never anticipate, but also makes connections to things that you may not have even considered. When you work on something that combines both the spectacular and the relatable, the hyper-real and the real, it suddenly can become supernatural. The hypothetical and the theoretical can become literal. And that is part of the genius of science-fiction or fantasy writing, which is that it suddenly lets you go, "Ooh – what if?" which the straight drama almost never lets you do.'

*Lost* was an idea that came out of nowhere, literally – the title of a script pitch to ABC by writer Jeffrey Lieber – and 'nowhere' because it was a happy accident of the meeting of like-minded individuals. Abrams was working on the script sent to him by the head of the network because the network chiefs were not too happy with the way it was developing. The pilot season for 2004 had already commenced and Abrams had received the script in January 2004. Burk met Abrams at a restaurant late one night, where Abrams showed him the script that he'd just been given. This sparked off a few ideas and the pair started talking about an island, just a random island, and what they could do with it in a story.

They continued the conversation the next day with some of their *Alias* writers such as Jeff McCurran and Jesse Alexander. The head of the network called him on the Friday and Abrams told him his thoughts about an island and how a show about an island would work. The head of the network was keen and asked Abrams to develop a show for him; but he was too busy with *Alias*. The network boss then said he'd bring in a writer, which he did. Damon Lindelof turned up on the Monday. Lindelof had been sent the same script and had the same ideas as Abrams and Burk, so the three of them began sketching out ideas throughout the rest of the week. Lindelof, who made an instant impression on Abrams, wrote an outline for the show and turned it in on the Friday, a week after Burk and Abrams had the meal together. The network chief reviewed the script and told them on the Saturday to make a pilot.

Carlton Cuse, whose credits include *Nash Bridges* and *Martial Law*, was brought in as executive producer and showrunner alongside Lindelof. The pair had met during the sixth season of *Nash Bridges* when Cuse had hired Lindelof and given him his first staff writer job. Cuse was brought in to help run *Lost* with Lindelof, who'd had no experience running a show, when Abrams went on to direct *Mission: Impossible III*.

Abrams was humble about his part in the creation of the show, and never took too much credit for *Lost*. 'I'm not just grateful that meeting Damon was sort of the catalyst for and the alchemy to create the pilot and series,' Abrams told *TV.com*, 'but that he and Carlton Cuse really took all the reins to run the show this year. I've been perfectly involved this season, but I'm as much a fan of theirs as anything.'

Lindelof and Cuse had a very productive partnership; they wrote over half of the episodes together and worked alongside each other in the writers' room taking part in rewrites, story meetings and even had input together on editing and casting.

Abrams, Burk and Lindelof have the same kind of passion, ideas and commitment and one of the best things to come out of *Lost* was their lasting friendship. Such were their mutual interests and the chemistry they had as writers and creative people that they stitched a TV show together virtually out of thin air within less than a week, when other shows were already being cast and prepped for a pilot episode ready to air later in the year. *Lost* was basically born out of the network's need to fill a slot in their TV schedule. It was an amazing, almost spontaneous act of creativity, as the pilot was made in less than eleven weeks. The two-part pilot episode of *Lost* cost between $10 and 14 million and was the most expensive episode in the network's history. They obviously had faith in it.

Other TV shows that were ratings hits in 2004 included *House*, *Entourage*, *CSI: NY*, *Boston Legal* and *Rescue Me* but nothing gained the global appeal of *Lost*. It was really rather extraordinary.

Sid Smith praised the first season in the *Chicago Tribune*: 'Abrams and Lindelof have crammed this one with so many chills and cliffhanging plot twists that it's all about sitting back, tossing credulity out the window and waiting for what happens next. The classy look and feel of the opener (the series is shot in Hawaii) also help make *Lost* a feast for the young and young at heart, even if you find yourself a little embarrassed, in the dead of a dark Wednesday night, to be so seduced by Saturday matinee fare.'

The writers and producers kept up to speed with fan reaction online by checking blogs and fan sites. 'It's funny because when we did *Lost* we would just gravitate towards things that people didn't like or things that were confusing,' Burk told *Digital*

*Spy*'s Simon Reynolds. 'Even when talking to J.J., he will say, "What didn't they like?" It's not looking for affirmation as much as it is seeing if people are not liking something.'

Abrams also composed the opening theme music just as he had done previously with *Felicity* and *Alias*. *Lost* ran for six seasons from 2004 to 2010 with 121 episodes. It drew inspiration from *Twin Peaks*, the eerie two-season cult TV show (completed by the 1992 prequel film *Fire Walk with Me*) by cult director David Lynch. Another influence on *Lost* was the extraordinary sixties British allegorical psycho-drama-spy-science-fiction mashup, *The Prisoner*, starring Patrick McGoohan.

'You know, working on *Alias* and *Lost*, which have both been incredibly rewarding and fun, you're right, has always been about how do we do this with that. How do you make this with that?' Abrams said to *About.com: Hollywood Movies*' writer Rebecca Murray. 'And the idea of taking the parameters of TV – the money, the schedule, the resources – and make something that hopefully looks filmic, it was great training.'

Working on *Lost*, Abrams learned how to delegate. He'd once been a micromanager and juggled writing, producing, directing, editing and even created the musical scores himself, but he found it impossible to do everything on such a high-concept production as *Lost*. 'He has to have six or seven things going on to activate him. It energises him creatively,' said Damon Lindelof to *USA Today*'s Bill Keveney.

*Lost* has since become one of the most popular, confusing, frustrating and talked-about TV shows of all time. It combines action and adventure with science-fiction, supernatural and religious themes. The basic premise is the experience of the survivors of the crash of a commercial passenger plane flying between Sydney and Los Angeles. They crash-land on a mysterious island somewhere in the South Pacific Ocean. The series was filmed on location in Oahu, Hawaii and stars such well-known TV actors as Matthew Fox – who had made a name for himself in the San Francisco-set drama *Party of Five* – Michael Emerson and Terry O'Quinn. Evangeline Lilly was a complete unknown. They had auditioned more than sixty women for the role of Kate but after noticing Lilly they knew she was the one straight away.

In 2006, Abrams was asked for his thoughts on the possibility of making a *Lost* film, which fans no doubt would love to have seen become a reality. He told *IGN*'s Stax: 'I think we make it every week. I honestly do not know what else we would do, but there have been discussions of sorts of all different types of things in *Lost*, but it feels like to me that the ambition at least in the production in that series is to try and make a little movie every week.'

Abrams's literary hero Stephen King had tried serialising his novel *The Green Mile* to powerful effect and Abrams wanted to try something similar on television. Such a style of storytelling goes back to the Victorian novels of Charles Dickens or the short stories of Sir Arthur Conan Doyle, creator of Sherlock Holmes. 'It's a leap of faith doing any serialised storytelling. We had an idea early on, but certain things we thought would work well, didn't. We couldn't have told you which characters would be in which seasons. We couldn't tell you who would even survive,' he explained to *The Guardian*'s Steve Rose in 2009. 'You feel that electricity. It's almost like live TV. We don't quite know what might happen. I'm sure when Charles

Dickens was writing, he had a sense of where he was going – but he would make adjustments as he went along. You jump into it, knowing there's something great out there to find.'

During its peak seasons *Lost* consistently drew 16 million viewers in the States. It was a bona fide hit and ABC had another winner to set alongside *Desperate Housewives*. 'He manages to maintain an almost childlike thrill to what he's doing,' said ABC program chief Stephen McPherson to *USA Today*'s Bill Keveney. 'I was working with him on the opening for *Alias*, and he's showing it to me like it's the first piece of film he ever shot.'

Such was the success of *Lost* and the mystery surrounding its premise that it has spawned a whole literature on the mythology of the series and its recurrent themes. *Lost* has also been parodied many times including spots on *The Office*, *Family Guy*, *The Simpsons* and *American Dad*. The writers kept as much as possible a mystery. The actors were often kept in the dark, but they did go to the writers if they felt something was unrealistic and wasn't going to work. 'Don't assume that we all didn't know what was going to happen,' lead star Matthew Fox admitted to *Time*'s James Poniewozik. 'I actually had some in-depth conversations [with Damon Lindelof] early in the season about it, so I could have some kind of understanding of what was going on.'

Through the years *Lost* won numerous awards and nominations and is often ranked as one of the best TV shows of all time by pundits, though it often infuriated many viewers and critics. Fox spoke to *The Guardian*'s Ryan Gilbey about the show's enduring appeal: 'The answer to any question can be found on Google. But just as all the Internet was catching on, you had *Lost*, which fed on the exact opposite part of human nature: the side that wants desperately for there to be an incredible, unknowable mystery in our lives and our souls. Everyone gravitated toward this show where no one knew what the fuck was going on. You couldn't Google the answer.'

The series grabbed a generation of viewers in a way few TV shows manage to do. Even viewers who were not especially fond of genre shows were seduced. It certainly marked its creators as some of the most imaginative and talented people working in TV and J.J. Abrams had become something of a household name. There is no doubt that Abrams had become the Steven Spielberg of his generation – with his hand in various media endeavours and his head in all creative processes. And much like Spielberg, Abrams's name has become a brand whereby movie goers or TV fans know which are his productions. Now, *that* is success! Abrams had next to nothing to do with the day-to-day running of *Lost* as it was left to Damon Lindelof who ran the show from partway through the first season. Abrams was busy working on movies; he watched the episodes and read the scripts but that was about it. He watched the show as a fan; not as someone involved with it behind the scenes (with one brief return to co-write the third season curtain-raiser).

The writers and producers kept the script for the final episode a closely guarded secret. A script could never be left with a third party. The production crew member took care of it and made sure only a limited amount of people got to see it. They even kept a piece out of the final script that was the linchpin for the episode and not every actor was permitted to read it.

Abrams spoke to Peter Sciretta of *Slasher Film* about the controversial ending: 'We had a lot of discussions about what the thing could be, and we knew that we had a few interesting ideas. It was everything from a creature that had been factored into a security system to…we discussed a bunch of things. All of them kind of had full possibilities…And as we were writing it we discussed things, when we were shooting it we discussed things, when we were cutting it we discussed things, but we didn't have a bible written of what the show would be, like any series. And anyone who tells you otherwise is not being honest. You cannot know every single answer. You have big ideas that give you a roadmap, and you can have a willingness to take that leap of faith, you are going to find it. But we did not have, in any way, every answer.'

He continued: 'At the time we knew specific things that we felt it was where the show needed to go. But when you think about things like Ben is not a character in the pilot, we didn't know he was going to show up. But you think of how critical he was and what the others said and what his relationship was to the whole cast. It just shows you how the show, any show, evolves over time. So what Damon and Carlton and the others came up with as they worked on the show was never anything that we could have known after we did the pilot. But you go into it knowing as much as you can and believing that you've got a sense of what there's going to be. What it ends up being is always different, sometimes very close, sometimes as far away as you can imagine from those real ideas. But you go into it with at least a bag of best ideas you've got, but you are well aware that as you travel down that path, if you are lucky enough to stay on the air, that bag of best ideas is going to shift, sometimes entirely.'

The ending was the cause of anguished debate amongst fans,

some of whom felt that is was predictable and lame. Mike Hale of *The New York Times* wrote that 'The End' was 'shaky on the big picture – on organising the welter of mythic-religious-philosophical material it insisted on incorporating into its plot – but highly skilled at the small one, the moment to moment business of telling an exciting story. Rendered insignificant... were the particulars of what they had done on the island.'

Indeed, Hale was not the only critic to give a lukewarm response to the ending, which displeased many critics. Alan Sepinwall of *Star-Ledger* was less than enthused: 'I'm still wrestling with my feelings about "The End"... I thought most of it worked like gangbusters...But as someone who did spend at least part of the last six years dwelling on the questions that were unanswered – be they little things like the outrigger shootout or why The Others left Dharma in charge of the Swan station after the purge, or bigger ones like Walt – I can't say I found "The End" wholly satisfying, either as closure for this season or the series...There are narrative dead ends in every season of *Lost*, but it felt like season six had more than usual.'

However, Richard Vine, writing in *The Guardian*, was more satisfied: 'It does feel like a decent enough finale – and, aside from Vincent being there is what Lost In Lost predicted at the start of this season: Jack closing his eyes. But while it was highly entertaining, and packed with great lines and moments, it's hard to escape the feeling that it's not quite an ending that matches our jumping-off point six years ago. Maybe that's the point: it's been a great ride, but now it's time to let it go to the great box set in the sky…where we'll doubtless find another twenty minutes of extra stuff to cry and argue over.'

For years people had been praising *Lost* to death but ultimately the ending infuriated them because they felt cheated. They felt that they had wasted years on a show that failed to deliver the ending they wanted. There were some people who were just upset that it ended but there were certainly others who were upset with the way it ended. In many people's eyes, the ending of *Lost* sucked.

'I'm satisfied with the finale,' Jorge Garcia, who played Hurley and later cropped up in the Abrams-produced TV series *Alcatraz*, said to *Time*'s James Poniewozik. 'I think both storylines that were introduced in the season, the finale wraps them up well. They make a bold choice. Anytime you do that on a show like this, we know what we're gonna get – the reactions will be mixed. It'll be interesting hearing the reactions over the summer. It's nice not being a writer around here when finale time comes around.'

What did Abrams have to say about 'The End'?

'If you were looking for some kind of technical explanation, you had missed the point,' he said to Andrew Collins of *Radio Times*. 'How you could look at that ending, which was beautifully rendered, and not find it wonderful and satisfying is beyond me. I believe that if people didn't like the ending, they didn't like it because it was gone.' (Oh, and what was 'The End'? Well if you didn't see it you won't get a spoiler here. You don't even get to know on Wikipedia. As Ryan Gilbey wrote, 'You can't Google the answer.' You can in fact, but you have to work at it.)

Disney, who owns the rights to *Lost*, have since expressed interest in a spin-off series or film, though Lindelof and Cuse have stated they wanted *Lost* to be a stand-alone series and have no interest in returning to the show. *Lost* may have J.J.

Abrams's name on it but he took a back seat while Lindelof and Cuse ran the show, and Abrams actually worked on other projects throughout its entire six-year run.

CHAPTER 5

# DOMINATING HOLLYWOOD

'The sound is always absolutely critical…'
**J.J. Abrams, *Movies Online*, 2009**

Bad Robot Productions, as it became known, had moved to Paramount Pictures and Warner Bros. Television in 2006 after its contract with ABC came to an end. Bad Robot Productions has since become one of the most successful and prolific production companies in Hollywood. 'Actually, I'm fascinated by robots,' Abrams explained to *The New York Times* regarding the company's moniker. 'I have this small collection of old tin toy robots and a wonderful robot painting…I love the idea of anthropomorphising machines. I love the idea of taking technology and giving it a personality.'

Its famous production logo was first shown back in 2001. A stylistic silhouetted piece, it features a red, rectangular-headed robot running through a meadow until it appears right in front of the camera. Two voices at the end say 'Bad Robot', those of Abrams's two children Henry and Gracie. Some Abrams fans assumed that the title comes from a line in the cult animated film *The Iron Giant*, though Abrams squashed that notion after he said in an *Entertainment Weekly* interview that it came to him during a writers' meeting one day. Bad Robot Productions is based in Santa Monica, California. There have been ideas to develop a Bad Robot movie based on the character seen in the logo, but it was originally developed as a children's book so they would probably start with that first.

At the Bad Robot offices Abrams created a recording area that quickly became his retreat; it contains a keyboard, guitars and a computer.

'All I know is that since working together on *Alias*, the four of us, and then with Damon on *Lost*,' Abrams said to *Movies Online*'s Sheila Roberts, 'when you work with people that you love, when you have a great shorthand and you appreciate similar kinds of things, it's not to say that you don't want to do comedy. These guys have written and produced things that have nothing to do with genre. Bryan and I have produced things that don't. I've written things that don't. But we also have to love that stuff. We all look at it as a fun collaboration. Again, I just hope I'm lucky enough to keep working with these guys on whatever it is because it's fun.'

In 2006, during the final season of *Lost*, he served as executive producer for the ABC show *What About Brian*. Created by Dana Stevens, the series concluded in 2007 after just two seasons. 'Pitching is always a weird, difficult thing,' Abrams confessed to Abbie Bernstein of *Assignment X*. 'At the very beginning, you just need to make sure that you have a handle on the characters and the potential of those characters. If you know what you want is really, really weird stuff, keep it to yourself.'

*What About Brian* is about a thirty-two-year-old man named Brian Davis who enjoys the single life in Venice Beach, California but he is the only single man within his group of friends. Reviewing the season in the *Chicago Sun-Times* Doug Elfman said: 'There's peril in traveling the well-worn path of unrequited love and adulterous wives. But what makes this beginning of "Brian" work is that the characters are nicely drawn archetypes, not stereotypes.'

Abrams also executive-produced *Six Degrees* for ABC, which was created by Raven Metzner and Stuart Zicherman. The series is about six residents of New York City and their relationships and how they deal with what life throws at them. It ran for just one season; five episodes were unaired due to low ratings. Revolving time slots, which often kill a show, didn't help. Adam Buckman wrote in the *New York Post*: 'It is no small feat to pull off the trick of interweaving so many characters and storylines, but the producers of *Six Degrees* have accomplished it with admirable smoothness for a series that is just getting under way.'

Abrams was not an overnight success like his hero Steven Spielberg, whose feature-length directorial *Duel* became an instant classic in 1971; though it was a made-for-TV-movie, it did get a small theatre release and has since become considered a minor gem in Spielberg's glittering back catalogue of films. *The Sugarland Express*, his first proper theatrical directorial debut, was released in 1974 to good reviews, while his third film *Jaws*, released in 1975, practically turned him into a celebrity. The haunting John Williams score, the powerful lead performance by the late Roy Scheider and some Hitchcockian camera tricks helped turn a modestly budgeted film into a huge box-office success. Spielberg would then go on to make some genre-defining films that influenced an entire generation, and no doubt subsequent generations, of film directors, writers and producers. *Close Encounters of the Third Kind*, *Raiders of the Lost Ark*, *E.T.* and *Jurassic Park* define an era of filmmaking, one which, it can be argued, is long gone, given how bloated and emotionally detached modern blockbusters are.

Abrams was part of a new generation of filmmakers who were tech literate and computer savvy; they are the bridge between old and new Hollywood; at the forefront of technical innovations and attuned to social media. Abrams was in the new school of Hollywood filmmaking.

After years in TV, Abrams ventured back into mainstream Hollywood movies with *Mission: Impossible III* starring Tom Cruise. It was Abrams's film directorial debut. Similarly to his hero Spielberg, Abrams had learned to direct by working in television. TV is much harder in some ways than making a film because you might be dealing with eight to a dozen or more episodes on a tight time scale and budget; and the days are long.

'…I did *Felicity*, it was the first thing that I directed, not the pilot but I did an episode of it, two episodes,' he said to one interviewer at *Salty Popcorn* when asked about how he directs actors once they're on set. 'It was great because they were these kids…twenty something; I was in my late twenties, they were early twenties and it was…they weren't intimidating at all, because I knew them and I had worked with them for months and it was like you know, oh Carrie and Scott you know, then when I wrote *Alias* and I did *Alias*, and I knew Jennifer Garner from *Felicity*, but we cast Victor Garber and Ron Rifkin and on the first day of working with them I was really intimidated, because these were, like, adults.'

With *Mission: Impossible III* Abrams would enter the big league of Hollywood players. *Mission: Impossible II* was released in 2000 and the sequel was already in development but it was going through a tough time. *Se7en* and *Fight Club* director David Fincher was initially slated to take the directorial reins for the third film in the franchise for a summer 2004 release, but declined in favour of another project. It was later reported that Fincher left the project over creative differences, which is not uncommon in Hollywood. Joe Carnahan, director of the 2002 film *Narc* starring Ray Liotta, took over and spent fifteen months developing the project. The film was set to star Kenneth Branagh, Carrie-Anne Moss and Scarlett Johansson. Thandie Newton was asked to reprise her role as Nyah Nordoff-Hall from the second film but she declined the invitation. Carnahan left the project in July 2004 after disagreements over the tone and style of the film. That same year writer/director Frank Darabont, best known for the Stephen King adaptions *The Shawshank Redemption* and *The Green Mile*, wrote a screenplay for the third film. Cruise would then eventually enlist Abrams, whom he had met previously with Paula Wagner (co-producer).

'We had talked about doing *War of the Worlds*,' Abrams told *Wired* writer Jennifer Hillner. 'The idea of getting involved with Tom Cruise and Steven Spielberg, who is my idol, was huge, but I had *Lost* coming up. So I thought, well, there goes my career.'

'Within the first couple of minutes I knew I liked him,' Cruise said to *IndieLondon*'s Jack Foley about when they first met in the early 2000s. 'I knew of his work but just as importantly I liked him, he's very charismatic and smart. Then something just happened creatively and we started working together.'

'I felt like it was an episode [of] *Punk'd*,' Abrams said to *Entertainment Weekly*. 'We had this two-hour meeting. I had known Steven for a few years, but it was always an out-of-body experience, and so to compound it with having Cruise on the same sofa, it was freaky. It was really fun, Tom and I got along great…'

'As I was leaving,' Cruise continued to tell *IndieLondon*'s Jack Foley, 'his secretary came out and gave me the first season of *Alias* which I'd never seen before. One night, I was up at my ranch in Colorado and I put the *Alias* tape on. I started watching the pilot, which J.J. had directed, and I was blown away. I put the next one and the next one and I ended up watching as much as I could. Within a couple of days I had finished the whole first season and I called him on the phone – he was actually on set in Hawaii shooting *Lost* – and said: "I couldn't turn it off. That was brilliant. Call me when you get back to LA." So I met with him and I went in the editing room and he showed me a couple of scenes from *Lost* which I thought was incredible. I said: "Look, when are you going to direct a movie?"'

Cruise invited the then CEO of Paramount, Sherry Lansing, (wife of *The Exorcist* and *The French Connection* director William Friedkin) over to his house for dinner with Abrams to talk about the movie. Abrams eventually signed on to direct the film, though production was delayed by twelve months due to his obligations to the final season of *Alias* and the first season of *Lost*, which left the Paramount bosses stressed over the film's release date and their production schedule. Because of Abrams's schedule the most challenging aspect of the film for Cruise and Abrams was actually trying to convince Paramount to hand Abrams the franchise for the third film. Branagh, Moss and Johansson had passed because of the delays in production. Paramount were keen to get it in cinemas as quickly as possible, and a new cast was hired after Paramount finally green-lit the film in June 2005.

Now with backing from Paramount and with Cruise firmly committed, Abrams jumped at the chance to direct the film. His answer was an immediate yes, I'm on-board! 'When Tom offered me the movie, it was the most unexpected thing – on every level,' he told Clint Morris of *Web Wombat*. 'The weirdest thing was, I had gotten to know Tom, we had become friends, and he had never brought it up. I mean…I knew he was getting ready to do *Mission Impossible*, and I thought maybe he might ask me to help with the script, or something, if they had problems with it, but he gave me the impression there were no issues at all. He seemed quite happy with what was happening with it.'

A few projects had come up in the past offering the chance for Abrams to make his big screen directorial debut but they hadn't felt right, but *Mission: Impossible* was the perfect opportunity for him. It had taken so long to find a script that he'd worried whether he was lacking confidence. Abrams happily volunteered the fact that before he started making the film he called fellow director Cameron Crowe for advice on working with Cruise, as the pair had made two rather good films together: *Jerry Maguire* and *Vanilla Sky*. (Though the reviews for the latter erotic sci-fi thriller were decidedly mixed, with words such as 'narcissistic' and 'pretentious' being bandied about.) '[Cameron] just said, "Brother, you are going to be spoiled." I now know he was right. Tom is the hardest-working, most focused, generous, passionate-about-the-form collaborator I could imagine,' Abrams told the May 2013 issue of *Playboy*. 'I was a first-time feature director, and before we started shooting Tom said, "I'm your actor; you're the director." There was not a day on that movie when Tom was not supportive, encouraging, collaborative, excited. He never mandated anything. He never insisted on things going a certain way.'

The idea of jumping into an already popular franchise and making something new and fresh was a challenge but one which Abrams relished. It was akin to James Cameron coming along and directing *Aliens*, the popular 1986 sequel to Ridley Scott's revered 1979 first film, *Alien*. It was part of the series yet something completely different. Some say it's better than the first film; others disagree. Importantly, *Aliens* was a different production from *Alien* and so with *Mission: Impossible III* Abrams wanted to make a different film, yet have the *Mission: Impossible* stamp on it.

'Not only was I being given the chance to direct a movie, it was a movie that included so many of the things I loved: espionage and action and comedy and scope and scale,' Abrams enthused to *The Guardian*'s Andrew Pulver.

With the third film, Abrams wanted to make the film as focused on the story as possible before even considering any special effects or stunt sequences. Once he felt he had a solid story he then began to think about how he could bring it to the big screen and what possible effects he could use.

Abrams and Cruise shared a mutual love of the spy genre and

action films in general and wanted the best story for the film. Despite Cruise's enormous success there was no ego involved in the making of the film. They both got down to work. They both wanted to make a film that was worth seeing, something akin to an event. They didn't want people to watch it simply because it said *Mission: Impossible III* on the promotional posters. However, Abrams, although impressed by the initial script, continued to have nagging doubts about its direction. '...When I saw the script that they were going to shoot,' he admitted to Jack Foley of *IndieLondon*, 'as brilliantly written as it was, I knew it wasn't a movie that I could do justice to. I knew it wasn't a version of the film that I could deliver – just because it wasn't what interested me. That's not to say it wouldn't be a great movie...it just wasn't the version that I felt like I could say to them: "I'm the guy for this..." So then I realised that I was in a very awkward position because I was being given an opportunity to direct this movie but I didn't want to direct the movie they were going to make.'

Abrams was desperate to direct a big screen movie but the offer to work with Tom Cruise on *Mission: Impossible III* was not the only reason why he accepted. He felt that though the first two films were well made they had not yet properly defined the franchise. Sure, some felt the first film was one of the best spy movies in recent years while others may have felt that the second film was one of the best action movies of the decade but Abrams wanted to properly realise the maximum potential of the series. He saw potential in making bigger and better *Mission: Impossible* movies.

Abrams reiterated the point to *Wired*'s Jennifer Hillner: 'I really liked the original script but it was not something I could deliver. It was like, I love the Bible, but I couldn't have written that. It was very intense, very dark. I wanted to do a movie that was about the home life, the truths a spy deals with. What's it like to come home to a partner who can't know what your job is? It's what got me excited about doing *Alias* – it's where the absolutely extra-ordinary, unexpected, and super-secret meets the absolutely mundane.'

When Abrams read the initial draft he felt there was something about it that just didn't sit properly with him; it was cool and everything but it wasn't right for him. It was not the film he wanted to make on a personal level and Abrams has to find a personal connection with his projects. He told Cruise his thoughts and assumed the actor would shrug his shoulders and move on to find another director; but Cruise asked him what he wanted to do. Abrams told him he had a more personal vision for the film. Cruise liked where Abrams was heading. He gave Abrams scope to do what he wanted with the script and did not offer a deadline.

'Tom said from the beginning that he wanted it to be "J.J. Abrams's *Mission Impossible*",' he said to *Web Wombat*'s Clint Morris. 'I was sceptical, it just didn't seem right for an actor or producer of his stature to let me do what I want, but he really did…he let me just go for it. He even let me cast the movie. For instance, I bought in Keri Russell, who I've wanted to work with again since we did *Felicity*, and I also brought my regular crew over – my editors, my production designers, my composer. He let me make the movie I wanted to make. All Tom had to do was to be a little bit of a jerk, a little less kind or even collaborative, and it could've derailed the whole thing.'

The original script wasn't Abrams's vision for the project so he roped in his buddies from *Alias*, Alex Kurtzman and Robert Orci, and started fleshing out an outline for a story that would work in an interesting and refreshing way for Abrams. It was a story about a spy but a spy who also had a home life. Plain and simple. Abrams felt that the audience would want to see how being a spy affected the character of Ethan Hunt personally. The completely revised script was written by Alex Kurtzman, Roberto Orci and Abrams. Kurtzman and Orci had become two of Hollywood's most successful screenwriters. They had moved into films from TV work after having rewritten the script for the Michael Bay-directed science-fiction movie *The Island*, which was released in 2005 and grossed $162 million. They then wrote the script for *The Legend of Zorro* before working with Abrams on *Mission: Impossible III*.

Another future frequent collaborator of Abrams was cinematographer Daniel Mindel, who was born in South Africa and educated in Australia and Britain prior to beginning his film career as a camera loader. He subsequently worked as a clapper loader and assistant cameraman on John Boorman's 1985 film *The Emerald Forest* working under the tutelage of French cinematographer Philippe Rousselot. He emigrated to America where he began working on commercials for Ridley and Tony Scott. Mindel worked as either a camera operator or photographer on a number of films for the Scott brothers, including the acclaimed *Thelma & Louise* (directed by Ridley) and *Crimson Tide* (directed by Tony). His next big break came in 1997 when he became the second unit director of photography on Ridley's *G.I. Jane* before becoming the director of photography on Tony's thriller *Enemy of the State* starring Will Smith, in 1998. Before being assigned as the director of photography of *Mission: Impossible III* he worked on *Shanghai Noon*, *Sand*, *Spy Game*, *Stuck on You*, *Domino* and *The Skeleton Key*.

Tellingly, Cruise took a pay cut – he was clearly hot for the new set-up – and the film's budget was redeveloped. The late, great Philip Seymour Hoffman, Ving Rhames, Billy Crudup and Simon Pegg joined Cruise. IMF agent Ethan Hunt would face his deadliest foe while trying to keep his identity clandestine to protect his girlfriend.

When casting, Abrams was looking for talented people who would not disappear in the superstar light emanating from Cruise, the other parts had to be strong to be seen. The actors had to be able to play on the same level as Cruise or it could break the film. Alongside the impressive line-up mentioned, Abrams also brought in the remarkable talents of Laurence Fishburne and Jonathan Rhys Meyers.

'The moment I met J.J, I knew he was going to take this movie and knock it out of the ballpark,' the Irish actor and model Rhys Meyers said to journalists at the 2006 WonderCon. 'There's not much of a difference shooting something for TV and shooting something for film. The difference is film is in a cinema and TV is in your home. J.J. has had a lot of success in television, probably the most successful guy in television, so it was very easy to make that transition from TV to film, really natural for him.'

He continued. 'It's all about the work. I'd work with a great director over… You know, I'm not the kind of actor who [says], "I want to play this role." It's more like, "I want to work with this director," regardless of what the role is because if it's a good director, you'll probably find a good role because it's a decent film. But a mediocre director will always make a mediocre movie.'

As for the female roles, Abrams brought in Michelle Monaghan and Maggie Q, and he even got to bring in Keri Russell who he'd worked with on *Felicity*. These actors have charisma, talent and charm. They helped make it a better film.

'What I loved about Jonathan Rhys Meyers,' Abrams said to *IGN*'s Stax on the film's casting, 'is he sort of felt to me in many ways the Irish version of where Tom was in the first *Mission* movie, which is a little bit more of a cocky guy who is at an age when he has not been doing this for very long. With Maggie Q, I really wanted to have an incredibly strong female and powerful voice and character, and someone who was as lethal as she is brave, and as she is vulnerable, and Maggie brought all that. She also looked incredibly good. That red dress that she wears to, of all places, the Vatican. I knew we had Ving [Rhames] coming back, who I had loved in so much of the work he had done in other films [including the peerless *Pulp Fiction*]. I felt like he still had not been as relatable as I wanted him to be in the first two films, and I just think he so brought an incredible personality to the role of Luther. So it was just important that Tom's character be surrounded by distinct and unique and compelling other characters.'

Abrams, a fan of the British zombie comedy *Shaun of the Dead* and the cult TV series *Spaced*, cast Pegg 'because selfishly I wanted to meet that guy. And I knew he would make any scene he was in better,' he explained to *The Guardian*'s Craig McClean.

Having used a strong female lead in *Alias*, Abrams hired Hawaiian-born Maggie Q, who was actually working in

Hong Kong when she took time out to fly to LA for casting. Abrams wanted a woman who could play at the same level as the men in the film. It's a testosterone-fuelled film but Abrams knew she was the right woman to hold her own. Maggie Q had worked under the tutelage of Jackie Chan in Hong Kong, where she trained with stunt guys on intense action scenes. She was prepared for the sort of training that was needed for *Mission: Impossible III*. 'J.J. is the kind of director – first of all, he's a director with no ego,' Maggie Q said to journalists at the 2006 WonderCon. 'He's a director who has a very consistent attitude when he's at work. He's funny, he's brilliant, and he's a combination of all these really great things. I always on the film had this sense of, you know, we're doing something special here…J.J. is the type of person who sees the bigger picture before anyone else does. It sounds simple, but not all directors do that.'

Tom Cruise also produced. Principal photography commenced on July 18, 2005 in Rome and ended in October with location filming taking place in Shanghai and Xitang in China, Berlin, Rome and Caserta in Italy, Vatican City and California and Virginia in the US.

The film has more than half a dozen major action sequences and Abrams worked them out on storyboards with storyboard artists. He knew that people who had seen *Felicity* would wonder if he could cope with a major action movie. 'I realised after the first few days this is a marathon,' he told journalists at the 2006 WonderCon, 'and the fun of doing this movie was being able to approach it the way I would approach making movies when I was nine, which was you look at a place, whether it's your backyard or down the street or a store, whatever, and you kind of figure out where's a cool place to put the camera.'

Abrams was often asked by journalists what it was like being a first-time director on a major Hollywood production. Tom Cruise had given Abrams the opportunity to sit in the director's chair of a film that was not only very costly but also hugely hyped. 'I mean he believed in me, and never wavered from that during the entire experience,' Abrams told *IGN*'s Stax. 'I do think that there were moments that I was in shock that I was given this opportunity, but the truth is I wanted to do this all my life. The pressure and experience of doing television seemed to continually confirm that doing a movie was something that was certainly possible. I did not necessarily think that the first movie I would get a chance to direct would be something as large as this one, but the crew was so incredible. Tom, and his producing partner, Paula Wagner were so supportive from the beginning that I always felt, and I believe the whole crew always felt, incredibly supported and safe, which always allows for more creativity. So the whole experience was great, and I honestly never doubted that I could do it. It actually felt incredibly comfortable doing it. It was a fun challenge.'

Cruise found working on the film to be a challenging experience, not just physically but also emotionally. Abrams had upped the ante by investing so much in the character of Ethan Hunt, who had become more reflective and honest in this film, rather than just your typical action hero as seen in the first two features. For Cruise, it didn't feel like he was working on the film of a first-time film director because of the sheer size of the production and how well organised it was. 'It's like when

I work with Steven [Spielberg],' Cruise told *IndieLondon*'s Jack Foley. 'There's never a moment where we are not going to figure it out, where it's not going to work. That's how I feel with J.J. – that we're always going to figure it out and come up with the ideas. You don't just write it and shoot it, you know. From a production standpoint, there are so many different elements and he handled it.'

Since the first film version, directed by Brian De Palma, had been released in 1996 much had happened to the spy genre, with movies such as the *Bourne* films starring Matt Damon breaking the mould and the James Bond films developing in a new direction with Daniel Craig, as well as popular TV shows such as *24* and *Alias*. Abrams was ambitious and wanted to make a movie that he would want to pay money to see on the big screen.

The visual effects in the third film are different from John Woo's second film in the franchise. Abrams discussed the effects with a group of online journalists at 2006's WonderCon, if somewhat obliquely: 'Some will be obvious because you'll think, "Oh, the scale of this or that," but a lot of the stuff is invisible. A lot of the stuff is stuff that we did so you won't know it's a visual effect, hopefully. [That] is the advantage of doing something like that as opposed to a *War of the Worlds* or something where you know the alien isn't real so you're kind of looking at it and, even if it looks absolutely for real, you're like scrutinising it almost unfairly. So the beauty of the visual effects in this, even though there are more than twice as many effects shots in this movie than in *War of the Worlds*, you'd never know it by looking at it.'

It was of course a big leap moving from *Alias* to *Mission:*

*Impossible*, not just with the size and scale of the production. There were a lot of things Abrams wanted to do with *Alias* which he couldn't because they never had the budget. The Vatican break-in sequence in *Mission: Impossible III*, for example, required a meticulous series of set pieces and a lot of time to set up; and time is something TV producers rarely have.

'And so working on this movie,' Abrams said at 2006 WonderCon, 'even though you think you have a hundred days instead of eight or you've got this budget instead of that budget, or you've got these sets or props instead of those, ultimately when it comes down to what's important in doing what I do, it came down to like the person right there and the camera. So that even though it's definitely massive, I mean the movie is sprawling in a lot of ways, it's only sprawling in so far as it's where the characters take each other. I don't think it's ever big for the sake of being big.' Abrams did not want to create an action scene or visual effect just for the sake of it; it had to be important to the progression of the story.

Having worked mostly in TV how did Abrams cope with large scale film sets? 'The thing is that going to the set every day,' he confessed to *About.com: Hollywood Movies*' writer Rebecca Murray, 'one of the things I realised really early on because at first I got there and I was like this is my first movie and there are more people working on the movie than had ever seen *Felicity*. I was like, "This is crazy!" And so I immediately started to try and figure things… By being too overly prepped or something, it actually gets in the way of that creativity because you go there and you go, "This is what I've decided it's going to be."'

First-time movie director J.J. Abrams was following in the

footsteps of masters Brian De Palma and John Woo. *Mission: Impossible III* is a different kind of film from the first two features. Whereas the first one was more plot and suspense, the second one more action, the third one is more personal and character-driven. It's tempting to say more 'realistic', in that the film generates its own internal realism. There is a lot of action in Abrams's film but it's not an action movie per se. There's a love story in there as well as comedy and emotion. Abrams used *Die Hard* as an example of what an action movie should be like – it's character-driven, which is why it remains so effective. The audience becomes invested in the characters, which they don't normally do in the typical Hollywood action flick.

Abrams was characteristically modest about his relationships with the actors. 'I was like "who the hell am I to tell an adult how to act", you know?' he told one interviewer at a Q&A press conference as quoted on *Salty Popcorn*. 'But I got through that; and then when I did the *Lost* pilot with Damon and we were doing that, it wasn't much about the actors, it was more the scale of that thing, but anyway from that I got *Mission Impossible* (3) and working with Tom [Cruise] it was…suddenly it was ridiculous, I was like, literally directing Tom Cruise…it was preposterous. Philip Seymour Hoffman; I am giving him notes. Lawrence Fishburne, I'm telling him how to do a scene. It was… it didn't make any sense! I was still the same as this idiot who did *Felicity* and there I am telling these real actors, you know, one of them who was the most famous person in the world, how I would like a line read…it made no sense!'

So Abrams began working out scenes in his head before a day's filming; knowing what he wanted on set and where he wanted the cameras to be placed. Overall, it was not a tough shoot for

Abrams. He found some of the emotional and intimate scenes more intense to shoot but the action sequences were fine.

Abrams thought it was a blast watching the actors use all the gadgets and gizmos and also seeing the story unfold, which is what was so compelling about the original TV series. The *Mission: Impossible* films required a certain degree of attention from the audience because the plots are so complicated and the technology is so elaborate, so Abrams was careful not to overload the audience with too much information.

'My mandate,' Abrams declared to *Wired*'s Jennifer Hillner, 'with all of the props was that they never feel like a magic computer that can do everything – which, by the way, I'm completely guilty of doing in *Alias* on more than one occasion. I wanted all of it to feel like real military field gear. There is classic spy gear and all that sort of paraphernalia, but it never supersedes who the characters are and what they're doing.'

There were inevitably spectacular scenes of physical daring in the first two films and that is something Abrams wanted to continue in his version (to be honest he never had a choice) so you get to see Cruise jump out of a building in Shanghai and leap off the tops of buildings and out of windows. It's all part of the fun of the franchise. Such acts of bravery are indicative of the extreme measures Ethan Hunt has to go through to succeed in his mission. They're old-school James Bond-type stunts and of course, there's always a woman involved. Ethan Hunt has certain characteristics in common with James Bond – he is good-looking, charming and dedicated to his job and is not afraid of getting his hands dirty on a mission.

Without wishing to labour the point, Abrams did not want to copy the first two films and his dream for his version was to see the agents as people and not just as spies, and this is reflected in a number of scenes. There was little seen of Ethan Hunt in the first two films outside of being a spy, aside from him climbing a mountain at the start of the second feature. Abrams was intrigued by the notion of seeing what Ethan Hunt was like when he went home and who the woman was in his life, so he chose to add humour and romance to the film. Abrams's belief – that you can have countless action scenes and explosions and thrills in a blockbuster movie but the main thing is always investment in character and story – comes through in the end product.

Abrams did not have a personal philosophy when it came to directing beyond making sure scenes were not over-acted or staged and were not redundant or filler material. Everything had to be integral to the story. Abrams had not yet had time to develop his personal style of directing – that would come in due course – for now his focus was on story. He wanted there to be spontaneity to the action scenes, thus making sure the audience could easily follow the characters throughout the film and know their motivations. 'The most important thing was that I tell the action sequences as if they were scenes of people talking,' he said at a press conference at the 2006 WonderCon. 'That you always knew where you were and why. A lot of times people say, "Oh, the geography of certain action sequences is hard to follow," or whatever. I think one of the reasons that that's the case is that sometimes the action supersedes character and story. It becomes about the moment, the stunt, the thing that you know they were planning for weeks and weeks and weeks and did tests and all that kind of stuff, then they put nine cameras down and filmed it and cut it together.'

*Mission: Impossible* was a high-concept show for its time, much like the *CSI* or *NCIS* of today, which creates little emotional attachment between the audience and the characters, but with more focus on story. Each of the characters had a role to play and the viewer got to see the relationship between them. Abrams chose to make a different kind of film from the first two features, though he did make a reference or two to the forerunners in his version. He approaches each film he directs with the same question 'Would I want to see this movie?' Abrams has always felt it is important to balance character with story and action because it is all-too-easy for action to dominate and therefore weaken the other two elements. He intended to give the audience what he believed they wanted to see, what he wanted to see: plot and action but with character development.

Tom Cruise famously handles stunts himself and writers Kurtzman and Orci wrote the script knowing how dangerous some of the stunts would be. Cruise is in fantastic shape and his physique is almost like that of a professional sportsman. John Woo talks about how frightened he was during the famous mountain-climbing scene in the second film and his anecdote became a constant warning bell for Abrams. Cruise would take care of his own stunts each day and not show signs of fatigue, whereas a professional stuntman trains and preps for weeks beforehand and performs just a handful of stunts for a film. Abrams was impressed by Cruise's tenacity and dedication to the job; he was professional and committed. But it was nerve-racking to be ultimately responsible for the well-being of the Billion-Dollar Man.

Cruise's stunt co-ordinator Vic Armstrong talked him

through the more difficult stunts, such as the scene where he is slammed into a vehicle after the villains fire missiles at his own car on a bridge. Abrams did not try to talk him out of doing the stunts, though Cruise knew he was going to be put to the test. He tried to get the stunts done in the lowest number of takes as possible. Cruise came up with some ideas for stunts just a day before they shot them, such as the one where he is sliding on the ground by a car. He got slammed around quite a bit and he even separated six ribs; three on each side. But, like Abrams, he was a hard worker and totally committed.

Vic Armstrong was incredibly supportive and his very presence made them breathe easier despite the danger of the stunts. Cruise is a very physical actor and knows exactly what he has to do and how he has to discipline himself to carry out such dangerous work.

'Yes, that was Tom running full bore and getting ratcheted and slammed into the car,' Abrams told *IndieLondon*'s Jack Foley. 'I have to say that the thing that excites me about Tom doing these stunts is not simply the idea that if you see this movie, you get to see him doing his own stunts – because I think although that's interesting to me, it's not a compelling reason to see this movie. The difference between Tom doing these stunts and our putting Tom's face on a stuntman in post-production, is that he is such a good actor that he is not just doing a stunt, he is performing a scene. So if you look at that scene where he goes slamming into the car, it's not great because he ran and got slammed into a car, it's great because if you watch his face, if you watch how he is running with such utter fear, he is selling the idea that a missile is literally about to blow up the car he is in. When he hits that car, his performance as he hits and then immediately after he hits, is as good as it gets.'

The logistics of filming in LA, Virginia, Italy, China and Berlin were inevitably daunting. But all the stunts and action sequences were finished ahead of schedule and under budget. However, Abrams also found the character work a challenge. He had Cruise play Hunt not just as a cool action hero but as a vulnerable human being. Stories of Cruise's personal life and of his dedication to scientology and his marriage to Katie Holmes (in November 2006 in a Scientology ceremony in Bracciano, Italy) had been making the newspapers but Abrams hoped that the audience was smart enough to differentiate between fact and fiction – and frankly, not to give a damn.

The actors were fully supportive of Abrams and his vision for the franchise. Ving Rhames spoke to journalists at the 2006 WonderCon about the future of his character: 'I would probably say we're on the right path. I didn't give them notes on how to expand my character in this one, but I think what the writers do, and I applaud J.J. for this, is that the more you see the main character interact with people around him, the more you learn about him. I would learn more about you by seeing your mother, your father, your daughter, your brothers, your cousin. I'm learning about you by how you relate to people close to you and how you relate to strangers. J.J. knew that as a writer. That's why we tapped into something that's a bit more human than the other two. I think we'll continue to go in that path.'

It was a hundred-day shoot and, as with any film, there were countless weeks spent on pre- and post-production, and while all that was happening Abrams was working on other projects. 'I wake up around 7 a.m.,' he told *The New York Times* of his morning routine, 'make breakfast for my children and take the older ones to school. Then I go to the office. Typically, I'm working on *Lost* and *Alias* at Disney, but these days I'm finishing up *M:I III* at Paramount.'

The film opened in the US on 5 May 2006 and received positive reviews from film critics. It made $16.6 million on its opening day of release and $47.7 million on its opening weekend, making it one of the highest grossing films of the year.

The famed resident *Chicago Sun-Times* film critic Roger Ebert wrote on his site: 'I saw *M:I* and *M:I II* and gave them three-star ratings because they delivered precisely what they promised. But now I've been there, done that, and my hope for *M:I IV*, if there is one, is that it self-destructs while mishandling the Anti-God Compound.'

'The film is credited to three young writers,' wrote Philip French in *The Observer*, 'the plot is not so much newly minted as *Bourne* again, and the first-time feature director J.J. Abrams (best known for the TV series *Lost*) has an eye for a cliché. In cinematic terms, he subscribes to the big bang theory of film-making rather than being a creationist and spectacular explosions occur every few minutes.'

In his lukewarm 1/5 review in *The Guardian* Pete Bradshaw was unenthused and said: 'Anyway, here we are again for a third jog around the *Mission Impossible* track and it's turning into a very tired experience. J.J. Abrams, the creator of TV's *Lost* and *Alias*, has been entrusted with the franchise as writer-director. The gadgetry has been scaled down, there are hardly any laptops, and not even all that many scenes showing the latex masks.'

Ian Nathan in *Empire* was also only moderately warm towards the film: 'An inspired middle-hour pumped by some solid action gives you an idea how good the franchise could be, but we now live in a post-*Bourne*, recalibrated-*Bond* universe, where Ethan Hunt looks a bit lost.'

Once the promotional rounds for *Mission: Impossible III* had finished Abrams was ready to move on to his next project. He was confident and capable enough now to handle something bigger and bolder. Unlike some filmmakers, he'd finished his first movie feeling very positive. 'Working with Tom is the least amount of effort,' Abrams told *IndieLondon*'s Jack Foley, 'it has truly been a dream collaboration. He has been so focused and professional and not just collaborative, but deferential. He let me write the movie with my co-writers, the movie I wanted to write, he let me cast it the way I wanted to cast it. He let me direct the movie the way I wanted to direct it, and he let me cut the movie the way I wanted it. I am forever grateful to him for this opportunity.'

Abrams was now a bankable director. Long gone were the days of struggling to sell scripts and moving from one small job to the next. He was in the big league, both in television and cinema.

He guest-directed an episode of the US version of *The Office* in 2007. That same year his friend and collaborator Roberto Orci was named by *The Hollywood Reporter* as one of the fifty most powerful Latinos working in Hollywood.

After *Mission: Impossible* Abrams quickly moved onto his next major feature, which he would write and direct. Abrams would collaborate with an old friend of his on a monster movie that would give Godzilla a run for its money. It seemed as though anyone involved with Bad Robot was pumping out pure gold.

CHAPTER 6

# THE NEXT SPIELBERG

'I want to spark people's imaginations...'

**J.J. Abrams, *GQ*, 2011**

The monster movie *Cloverfield* was released in 2008, produced by Abrams and Bryan Burk and written by Drew Goddard, who had begun his career as a staff writer on the cult Joss Whedon TV shows *Buffy The Vampire Slayer* and *Angel.* It was directed by Matt Reeves, another important figure in Abrams's life and work.

Matt Reeves was born in Rockville Centre, New York on 27 April 1966, but raised in LA. He met his lifelong buddy J.J. Abrams when he was thirteen years old (the pair showed their Super 8 movies on the public access television channel, as described earlier). Reeves had been making short films since he was eight. He later attended the University of Southern California where he produced the award-winning student film *Mr. Petrified Forrest.* He subsequently hired an agent and wrote a script which eventually became *Under Siege 2: Dark*

*Territory*, starring action hero Steven Segal. He graduated from college and directed *The Pallbearer*, his first feature and his first collaboration with Abrams, who produced the film. He then teamed up with Abrams for the TV show *Felicity* and other TV credits include episodes of *Homicide: Life on the Street*, *Relativity*, *Miracles* and *Conviction*.

Reeves was planning to write and direct *The Invisible Woman* but the schedule of the actress cast for the lead role clashed with the film's production so it was put on hold. Abrams had been putting together a major movie deal for Bad Robot and was doing TV work and features and had an idea germinating for a monster movie. Abrams and writer Drew Goddard had been talking about a story which they pitched to Paramount, who immediately said yes. The problem was there was no script, even though Paramount said they would put it into production. The studio loved the idea. 'Apparently Drew walked out of that meeting,' Reeves told *io9*'s Kevin Kelly, 'and turned to J.J., because they'd pitched it as if they had everything, and he said "J.J., that's all we have!" J.J. said, "No no, we're gonna do it."'

Goddard then wrote a sixty-page outline in January/February of 2007, which he termed a 'scriptment' because it was a script and a treatment in one document. Abrams told Reeves one time about his idea while he was working on *The Invisible Woman*. It sounded interesting but Reeves never thought he'd end up directing it. One day when Reeves was working on casting for *The Invisible Woman*, Abrams and Burk asked him if he'd be interested in directing this monster movie idea they had. Reeves read the outline by Drew Goddard and was intrigued by the concept of a big monster movie that was huge and scary, yet intimate and personal. Reeves loved the outline and took it further by talking about character approach to the story and visuals. The script read like an *Independence Day* style movie with an epic scope, but in fact it would turn out to be something very different.

'I said "Well, this is clearly a wall-to-wall visual effects monster movie,"' Reeves told *Den of Geek*'s Sarah Dobbs, '"Why are you thinking of me?" And they said, "Well, because we want it to feel real." And then I was like, "Yeah, I get it, that sounds like fun." And for me it was.'

Reeves had never worked with visual effects before, as his background was in TV dramas and scriptwriting. He worked closely with Double Negative, the special effects company who had also been responsible for the effects in the 1997 Paul Verhoeven film *Starship Troopers,* adapted from a Robert A. Heinlein novel, to achieve his ambitions for the film. The idea essentially for *Cloverfield* was to make a monster movie that was epic in size, terrifying in its approach to the audience yet also intimate and naturalistic. With Reeves's background on *Felicity*, a small and intimate TV show, he was the right man for the director's chair. Despite being built around a 350-foot monster that is going to destroy the Big Apple, the film feels very personal because it is about the characters rather than, say, the military might of the US government, which is so common with American monster movies such as *King Kong* or the 1998 *Godzilla* remake, or even the disappointing *Jurassic Park* sequel, *The Lost World. Cloverfield* is nothing like a linear narrative about a monster attack on New York City as it is told from the point of view of a small group of characters. The idea for a monster movie dated back to a visit Abrams made with his son to a toy shop in Japan during the promotional rounds for *Mission: Impossible III* in 2006. Abrams saw some *Godzilla* toys and thought instantly that there should be a new American monster: something to rival the mighty *King Kong*.

The film was green-lit in February 2007 by Paramount Pictures but kept under wraps from the public. Abrams drew inspiration from the poster of the 1981 cult classic *Escape from New York* directed by John Carpenter, which featured the severed head of the Statue of Liberty. Further inspiration came from the original *Planet of the Apes* film released in 1968.

'One of the things we talked about when we were working on the story,' Reeves told *Ain't It Cool* writer Capone, 'Drew and I and J.J. were saying, Okay, the idea is that we have a traditional story, a traditional exposition in a certain way. And now that we know what the story is, we have to find ways to submerge it, so it doesn't happen in a way…one of the challenges of the movie is that you never want it to feel like the camera was in the right place at the right time for all of the information that you need, all the beats that you need, the action that you need. We were constantly finding ways to catch back up, to let things happen that were off camera and then get them on camera, and catch things not at the right moment.'

Apocalyptic tales have been a cinema staple for decades, most notably in the 1950s with the threat of communism during the Cold War. B-movies, monster movies and science-fiction films were allegories for the Red Menace. These movies echo social fears and anxieties and some of the best told science-fiction tales have always been about the present rather than the future, albeit wrapped up in futuristic aesthetics.

Abrams's hero Rod Serling dealt with all sorts of issues in

*The Twilight Zone*, from race to politics and various social concerns. He made the censors uncomfortable because of his boldness and he was doing a noble thing by bringing those issues to the forefront. 'With *Cloverfield* we were trying to create a film that would be entertaining and, as a by-product of the subject matter, perhaps be a catharsis,' Abrams told *Tech Land*'s Lev Grossman. 'We wanted to let people live through their wildest fears but be in a safe place where the enemy is the size of a skyscraper instead of some stateless, unseen, cowardly terrorist.'

The threat of attack became a reality for America on 11 September 2001. Suddenly, the villains were not monsters but real life people – terrorists. *Cloverfield* is a different sort of movie; it's a fantasy. It is pure entertainment. There is no hidden message; it is not an allegory with a deeper meaning, it's just a monster flick. But it is a well-made one.

In setting the film in New York after 11 September, they were making a controversial move. Would movie goers really want to see a film about a monster destroying the city after the horror of the Twin Towers attacks? But how do you tackle your fears and anxieties if you don't face up to them? (Perhaps 'tackle' is the wrong word: explore, touch upon, redirect or even displace maybe.) When *Godzilla* was first released in the 1950s, the idea of seeing a film about a radioactive man-made creature after the nuclear bombings of Hiroshima and Nagasaki in Japan did not appeal to everyone; it was just too close to reality, yet it's merely a man in a rubber suit. Pure entertainment. However, it was a way of touching on fears similar to the way modern-day films set in post 9/11 New York tackle modern-day fears about fundamentalism and terrorism. They could have set the film in Chicago or San Francisco but New York is the most recognised city in the world. There had been other recent movies, albeit pre 9/11, set in New York City, such as the awful 1998 *Godzilla* remake directed by Roland Emmerich, the disappointing *I Am Legend* starring Will Smith and the overblown remake of *King Kong* directed by Peter Jackson of *The Lord of the Rings* fame, so *Cloverfield* was not the only film to show off Manhattan's beauty while destroying it.

'For me, it's the idea of the bigger they come the harder they fall,' Abrams said to *Tech Land* contributor Lev Grossman on the topic of end-of-the-world films. 'The idea of seeing the *Titanic*, the unbreakable, unsinkable ship go down. Whenever a toddler sees a pile of blocks, he wants to tear it down. *Cloverfield* takes the incredibly familiar and relatable, and it adds an element of the absolutely fantastical. It's like in *Planet of the Apes*: When you see the Statue of Liberty on the beach, you realise that this creepy and compelling story happened where I live.'

Filming and casting was kept under wraps even more tightly than it is for most films. They didn't even have a script until four weeks before shooting. Abrams did not want any plot information leaked, so the actors auditioned with scenes from scripts from Abrams's previous productions such as *Alias* and *Lost*. Some scenes were actually written for the audition process and then scrapped. The film stars Michael Stahl-David as Robert 'Rob' Hawkins, T.J. Miller as Hudson 'Hud' Platt, Odette Yustman as Elizabeth 'Beth' MacIntyre, Jessica Lucas as Lily Ford, Lizzy Caplan as Marlena Diamond, Mike Vogel as Jason Hawkins, Ben Fledman as Travis and Billy Brown as Staff Sgt. Pryce.

The actors would improvise a great deal throughout the film, though they were not aware of that during the audition process. In fact, they didn't know what they were auditioning for because they were not handed a script. Lizzy Caplan thought that because Abrams and Reeves had created *Felicity* together that she would be auditioning for a relationship-type film but with an improvisational style. It created a bond between the actors because there were no scripts and Reeves pitched the story to them in person. It was a huge mystery. The actors spent a great deal of time together as a consequence and became good friends.

The film was given a budget of just $30 million and featured no household names. Principal photography commenced in June 2007 in New York. The film was shot and edited in a cinéma-vérité style, which made it look as though it was captured with a hand-held camera with lots of jump cuts similar to those found in home movies and YouTube videos.

'Because the premise of the movie is that when this thing first happens,' Reeves explained to *Ain't It Cool*'s writer Capone, 'nobody knows what's going on. It quickly evolves into something very, very different than that, although not in terms of tone, because it continues that realism. Obviously they're in New York and they take this sort of journey to survive the evening against whatever this crazy huge thing is. At a certain point, they begin to realise what it is, in that there's this huge thing there, and survival becomes the order of the day. There's this way that the movie both reflects and deals with these fears in a certain way, to approach them, but in a safe way.'

The realistic aspect of the project was what attracted Reeves to the film; it wasn't your ordinary run-of-the-mill monster movie. There is a level of realism to the film despite the central fantasy plot. It was a challenge for the director and writers to make it seem as real as possible. Reeves was influenced by war documentaries and news footage that he checked out on YouTube. One influence was *The War Tapes* by Deborah Scranton, who gave handicams to troops to film in Iraq. There was a lot of footage on the Internet, from people in crisis during 9/11 to world conflicts, which Reeves drew ideas from. Anyone can film something today on a mobile phone, a camera phone or a camcorder. 'I watched a lot of really weird and disparate things,' Reeves said to *LAist*'s Julie Wolfson. 'I watched *Children of Men* [2006 science-fiction thriller, directed by Alfonso Cuarón] because of the continuous shot aspect of it, and I thought it was really amazing, the tension that they were able to build in that. I was so impressed because the camera was very eerie and almost Kubrickian. The camera was in the middle of the space – handheld and right in the action – but it was also detached. I watched *Alien*, *Jaws*, *The Shining*, movies that I've always loved that are creepy and scary.'

An important aspect of the film was the sound, devised by co-supervising sound editors Douglas Murray and Will Files and re-recording mixer Anna Behlmer. The monster's vocalisations were designed by Files, who went to great lengths to carve out a personality for it by expressing emotions through those vocals.

Another film which was an influence on *Cloverfield* was an old (1947) film noir piece called *Lady in the Lake*, a 'first-person' film, in which Raymond Chandler's famous detective Philip Marlowe *is* the camera. Mike Bonvillain, the director of photography, suggested Reeves look at the film because it would provide ideas on how to handle *Cloverfield* in a different way. 'Obviously they did it with a very, very heavy camera,' Reeves told *Den of Geek*'s Sarah Dobbs about *Lady in the Lake*, 'and in that case you're supposed to be the guy, so people are looking at the camera and having conversations... it's kind of like this noirish movie, it's sort of stilted in a way, even though it was very innovative for the time. But here there was an actual sort of precedent for what it was, which was that it's not that the camera is the character but the camera is the Handicam, so that part of it was really fresh to think about how to approach.'

The shaky style of filming, which was called 'La Shakily Queasy-Cam' by the late film critic Roger Ebert, caused motion sickness and nausea amongst some viewers and so cinemas placed warnings about the camera work and its effects front-of-house (which, if anything, probably helped sell tickets). Steven Spielberg saw an early cut of the film and came up with the idea of hinting to the audience the fate of the monster during the film's climax. This prompted the filmmakers to add a countdown overheard on the radio in the helicopter and the air raid sirens to acknowledge the Hammer Down bombing.

'It's meant to be a horror movie of its time in the same way that *Godzilla* was definitely a reaction to the anxieties of that time – you know, post-Hiroshima and Nagasaki,' Reeves explained to *IndieLondon*'s Rob Carnevale, 'it was very much a movie about the anxiety during the atomic age. We felt that in doing a monster movie for our country and of our time that it would definitely be reflective of the anxieties we all feel since 9/11. So that was definitely something we were aware of from the beginning, although at the end of the day we were also aware that what we were making was a fantasy. That [9/11 anxiety] was an entry point for the film, a way in, but ultimately what we made was a giant monster movie. I think that all the really interesting genre films, to me, tend to reflect the anxiety of the time in which they were made. The '50s Red scare films, and the way that Romero's *Dawn of the Dead* was said to be a reaction to Vietnam. So there's no question that we were aware of that and that it's part of the environment in which we made the film.'

Neville Page designed the monster and the idea was that it would have an evolutionary, biological look. He created a sort of wall of terror in his office with photographs of intestines, eyeballs and body parts. Reeves was fascinated by Page's creative process. Page was creating a monster based on reality. He didn't want the audience to know where the monster came from, which added an extra feeling of terror; a feeling of the unknown. They came up with the secret that the monster was a baby and had been separated from its mother so it was feeling high levels of anxiety, which sent it into a rage in an alien environment. The monster was only seen from the point of view of the local people, so the audience was seeing and experiencing what they were.

'Drew was still working on *Lost*,' Reeves told *io9*'s Kevin Kelly, 'and we were working on weekends and talking about how to rework the story, coming up with the structure of the flashbacks and all that stuff. It was all madly coming together because we knew that we had this release date, and we also knew we wanted to finish this teaser trailer and get it onto the front of *Transformers*.'

The teaser trailer was attached to the Michael Bay-directed summer blockbuster *Transformers*, based on the cult 1980s cartoon series, because of the high tracking numbers in July 2007. Reeves thought it would be interesting for the audience to see a trailer for a movie that was totally unheard of before a film that was hugely anticipated. They knew they didn't have a well-known cast and had no real obvious marketable aspects to the movie except for the element of surprise, which they used in the trailer. Reeves, like Abrams, realised that most audiences know everything about a film before they go to the cinema, so with *Cloverfield* they wanted to do it differently, to make it an event.

'The thing is, during prep, we were making the trailer,' Reeves said to *Ain't It Cool*'s writer Capone. 'And in a way, it was a certain kind of exercise in learning how to make the movie as well. Drew and I were...talking about story and working on character direction to take things in the direction they told me about when they brought me in. Because Drew was so interesting in character, we just had a ball. But during the week, we'd be preparing to make this trailer because one of the concepts, which was so exciting to all of us, was the way that today, you're so saturated with the media that there isn't almost anything that could come out that you don't have some awareness of. You see a trailer and you say, "Oh, yeah. I've heard of that movie" or "I know who that person is."'

They snuck under the radar with a small film and surprised everyone with something terrifying. They knew that *Transformers* would be a big box-office hit, which in itself created a mystery around *Cloverfield*. The trailer made the film take on a life of its own. They had the initial idea of releasing something else about a month after the teaser trailer but people were so interested and intrigued by the trailer, wondering what the hell this monster movie was, that Rob Moore, a chief at Paramount, came up with the idea of releasing something without a title on it. Having been told that they could not delete the obligatory 'This preview has been approved for all audiences by the MPAA' from the trailer, they went to the MPAA, who rate trailers and give specifics on what is and isn't suitable for the audience, and asked if it was possible to release a trailer without the title. They said no one had ever released a trailer without a title. Reeves and company were concerned, though, that *too much* marketing would ruin the film's chances because so much interest had been built up around it. It harked back to the time when no one knew anything about a movie until they saw it at the cinema. Everyone concerned with *Cloverfield* wanted its release to be an event as in the old movie-going days of the 1970s and 1980s.

'The thing we talked about a lot was the trailer for *Close Encounters*,' Reeves said to *LAist*'s Julie Wolfson. 'There was a great teaser trailer that sort of looked like weird documentary footage and there was this really scary, almost frontline-esque narrator and he was talking about different close encounters. When it ended you were like "What was that?!?" The idea of having that experience where, as a moviegoer, you could discover something – before the age of *Access Hollywood* and *Entertainment Tonight* and all the websites.'

The film was set for a January 2008 release and on 4 July, only a week into filming, they were concerned people would have had enough already, let alone by the time the film was released. Much of the viral interest was not coming from the Bad Robot offices but from film buffs keen to know what the movie was about. Bad Robot had actually held back for much of 2007 simply so audiences would not get bored and move onto another movie. *Cloverfield* was wrongly connected to the viral campaign EHWR (Ethan Haas Was Right) which was created by Mind Storm Labs to promote *Alpha Omega: The Beginning and the End*, an apocalyptic role playing game. 'I remember Bryan and J.J. and I turning to each other and saying, "What is that? We don't even know what that is,"' Reeves said to *LAist*'s Julie Wolfson. 'That's what happens when you confront people with a mystery. You can't be surprised if they start making connections that have nothing to do with you. That's exactly what happened. When I look at the message boards to see what's going on, and there will be somebody who has purported to have seen the movie and they'll give details – very specific details – that have nothing to do with the film. I think, "People are amazing!" It's fascinating and it's just something I've never really been a part of prior to this. I mean, we had online fans during *Felicity*, but it was very different.'

Reeves was influenced by *Jaws* and *Alien* in that at the death the viewer finally gets to see the full monster after a massive scale of destruction created during the climax. Skywalker Sound up in Northern California provided the perfect soundtrack, which added to the terror. Practically all horror films rely on an effective soundtrack to tap into the viewer's primal fears. In *Cloverfield* the audience is right in the middle of the action because of the camera work, as was the case in *Jaws*. Much like films such as *Children of Men*, *Cloverfield* was a big film with impressive special effects but was still able to create a real feeling of intimacy and an emotional connection with the audience.

'I think we all felt from the beginning,' Reeves said to *Ain't It Cool*'s Capone, 'that you would have a particular connection with the person who was filming it, who you would see for very little of the film, ironically. Of course that person's behind the camera, but he is your eyes and your guide, and you'd have this association with this group of people who you've come to know, but with this person behind the camera you'd have a very special relationship, and we feel actually that that is true. We hope that when people see the movie, they feel that way. People we've shown it to, that has been the case. That part of it was incredibly unique.'

In November 2007 a second *Cloverfield* trailer was attached to the Robert Zemeckis directed CGI film *Beowulf*, this time confirming the title. After the hype surrounding the original trailer the title of the film was changed frequently during production until it was finalised as *Cloverfield*. One suggestion was 'Greyshot', which comes from the archway the two survivors take shelter under during the film's climax, but audiences had become so familiar with *Cloverfield* that Matt Reeves decided to keep it. The title of the film indirectly comes from the exit Abrams uses to leave his Santa Monica office. The road which leads to the local airport was originally called Cloverdale Avenue. Writer Drew Goddard misheard Abrams during discussions and thought he said 'Cloverfield' and it just stuck. It sounds mysterious, edgy and distinctly governmental, a code word. Within the film itself, 'Cloverfield' derives from the designated government case for the events created by the monster. 'I mean the Manhattan Project was the A-Bomb,' Reeves said to *IndieLondon*'s Rob Carnevale. 'The idea that you would have a project called Cloverfield, or a file, and that it would be referring to a crazy, violent monster attack was very funny to us. It's so incongruous. It's almost pretty.'

It received a subtitle in Japan called 'Destroyer' which was chosen by Abrams. A Manga spin off called *Cloverfield/Kishin* ('Fierce God') was released in Japan.

Because there was a no-name cast and because the trailer was causing such a stir, there were all sorts of speculations. The problem then is that people start to make a movie out of their own in their head, which can lead to disappointment. It got people talking, though, and in an age where everything is accessible online, the old adage of 'less is more' rings true. Among the various rumours circulating on the Internet after the trailer was screened was the suggestion that the film was based on the supernatural and macabre works of H.P. Lovecraft, or a live-action adaptation of Voltron. Others thought that it was a *Godzilla* remake or a film spin-off of *Lost.* All this talk and rumours fuelled speculation for months as to the film's plot and added to the viral campaign instigated by Paramount. One comparison, which was almost inevitable, was with *The Blair Witch Project.* The general vibe around *Cloverfield* was that they couldn't afford to make a movie with visual effects, so they relied on the audience's imagination to see what's off screen. Obviously, though, Reeves had a budget, even it was modest and he could scare the hell out of the audience with a giant monster if he so wished.

Ultimately Abrams wanted *Cloverfield* to be the sort of movie he saw at the cinema as a kid growing up in LA in the 1970s. 'I hadn't seen anything that felt that way for many years,' Abrams told *Tech Land*'s Lev Grossman. 'I felt like there has to be a way to do a monster movie that's updated and fresh. So we came up with the Youtubification of things, the ubiquity of video cameras, cell phones with cameras. The age of self-documentation felt like a wonderful prism through which to look at the monster movie. Our take is what if the absolutely preposterous would happen? How terrifying would that be? The video camera, we all have access to. There's a certain odd and eerie intimacy that goes along with those videos. Our take is a classic B monster movie done in a way that makes it feel very real and relevant, allowing it to be simultaneously spectacular and incredibly intimate.'

With visual effects from the much respected Chantal Feghali, *Cloverfield* was an instant box-office success when it was released on 1 January 2008 in the US. It grossed $40.1 million on its opening weekend and it was the first film of the year to make over $100 million. The $30 million budget film was no flop.

'Certainly we didn't set out to make a franchise, we set out to make a good movie,' said a proud Drew Goddard to *Collider*'s Adam Chitwood. 'That was what we set out to do. But also, I love that world and that universe so if there was an idea that excited us enough and we felt like there was a reason to do it, we would do it.'

The film was greeted with positive reviews.

Anthony Quinn wrote in *The Independent*: 'The first of Abrams' canny manoeuvres is to cast actors who are largely unfamiliar, much as Paul Greengrass did in his airborne ordeal, *United 93*. This isn't a patch on the Greengrass film, but it understands the importance of getting the feel right. A famous face would throw its softly-softly approach way off-course, whereas a bunch of unknowns have a democratising appeal: the message is, these terror-stricken souls could be us.'

Olly Richards enthused in his five-star *Empire* review: 'There will undoubtedly be those who don't enjoy it, and some will have probably decided on that before seeing a frame. Anti-populist party poopers could very well pick apart the fact that the characters are archetypes and that there's no hidden depth beneath the fright (although you could pub rant for hours about political subtext). But unmissable cinema does not have to be about mellifluous dialogue, intricate framing or enriching the mind or soul.'

Manohla Dargis wrote in *The New York Times*: 'Like too many big-studio productions, *Cloverfield* works as a showcase for impressively realistic-looking special effects, a realism that fails to extend to the scurrying humans whose fates are meant to invoke pity and fear but instead inspire yawns and contempt. Rarely have I rooted for a monster with such enthusiasm.'

Writing in *The Daily Telegraph*, Sukhdev Sandhu was not bowled over: 'Abrams, Reeves and scriptwriter Drew Goddard, though, stake everything on their ability to create a fright-flick from the perspective of sidewalkers looking upwards. They know that news companies quite like the eyewitness authenticity of mobile-phone and digital-camera imagery.'

'Look, I'm not that bothered that the structure of the movie is lifted from *The Blair Witch Project*,' Peter Travers penned in his *Rolling Stone* review, 'we're watching digicam footage found in the aftermath of destruction. It's the YouTube-ification of

Hollywood – let it roll. What galls me is that Abrams, whose first feature was the underrated *Mission: Impossible III,* has gathered his TV team – director Matt Reeves, who worked with Abrams on *Felicity*, and screenwriter Drew Goddard, who toiled with Abrams on *Lost* and *Alias* – to create characters that literally define vacuity.'

*Empire* magazine named *Cloverfield* the fifth best film of the year and the French film journal *Cahiers du Cinéma* named it the third best. It was nominated for various awards. It was released on DVD with two alternative endings. Ideas have been thrown around about the possibility of a sequel but thus far nothing has been committed to by anyone.

Reeves expressed his thoughts on a sequel to *Film School Rejects*' Brian C. Gibson: 'Sure, if I think the movie that sort of came out of [*Cloverfield*] was compelling for all of us. This idea was so compelling to do and we had so much fun in doing it because we had never done anything like it. So I think we would want to find a similar challenge to this, to find it having its roots in this but be fresh and new because otherwise you are just repeating yourself.'

Fast-forward to 2010 and Reeves said to *I Am Rogue*'s Jimmy O.: 'You know what? I wish I could tell you something but I really can't because there really isn't any new news. J.J. [Abrams] is shooting *Super 8* right now, which I know is his real passion project, and I finished this. So I've been working on this for two years. And then Drew Goddard, who wrote *Cloverfield,* he just directed his first movie that he co-wrote with Joss Whedon [*Buffy the Vampire Slayer*]. So he has been busy too, so the three of us haven't really been able to collaborate to figure out what exactly it will be. I can only say that, we want to make sure that if and when we do it, it's because it is something we can be as excited about it as were making that one.'

They didn't want to make a sequel just for the sake of it and rehash the first film, which sequels ordinarily do; and they had to all come to a mutual agreement about the story. Goddard, who went on to direct the quirky Joss Whedon-scripted horror film, *The Cabin in the Woods*, told Brad Brevet of *Rope Of Silicon*: 'It's more about can we find *that* idea and can we get something that excites J.J., Matt Reeves and I? Because *Cloverfield* was very much a discussion between the three of us so I don't think anyone would want to do it without those three people.'

Abrams did hint at the idea of a sequel after Guillermo del Toro's *Pacific Rim* was released in 2013, but he was interested in seeing how the *Godzilla* remake from *Monsters* director Gareth Edwards did at the box office in 2014 before he even thought about discussing any potential ideas for a follow-up.

'The nice thing about working with a guy like J.J. and the power he has [is that] the studio's not gonna force him to do anything,' Goddard told *Collider*'s Adam Chitwood. 'He's been able to say, "We'll do it when we're ready. We're not gonna do it just because it'll help your bottom line, we're gonna do it because there's an idea that excites us." So that's informed our discussions, we don't feel like we have to [do it], so it's like, "Can we come up with something that excites us enough to do it?"'

*Cloverfield* was a great springboard for Reeves, who went on to direct the excellent *Let Me In*, a remake of the highly acclaimed Swedish modern-day vampire film *Let the Right One In*. 'You know I never would have guessed I would be making science-fiction and horror films,' he admitted to *Collider*'s Steve 'Frosty' Weintraub. 'That kind of stuff. They were the kind of movies that frankly as a kid scared the hell out of me and so I really had a hard time watching them…I never thought I would be making them and then after *Cloverfield* happened it obviously created a lot of opportunity for me to do those kind of films. I discovered the fun of genre is…you get to explore your fears and you get to use the metaphor of the genre – whether it's a giant monster or a…twelve-year-old vampire. Whatever it is, you can sink something underneath the surface and make a personal film under the guise of great fun romp.'

*Cloverfield* wasn't the only project Abrams had been working on: in 2008 he also served as co-creator and executive producer of the science-fiction series *Fringe*, which ran until 2013. Created by Abrams, Alex Kurtzman and Roberto Orci, *Fringe* lasted for five seasons and a hundred episodes and was further evidence of Abrams's knack for connecting with audiences and making a hit series. *Fringe* ultimately became a mini franchise of sorts with a comic book series and various bits of memorabilia and paraphernalia to accompany the TV show.

Abrams is fascinated by the idea of mysterious boxes, sort of like Pandora's Box, and what they contain. It is something that fuels his imagination and creative drive. 'But the funny thing about the box motif is, it's just human nature, I think,' he said to Debbie Chang of *BuddyTV*. 'You want to know, what is it? What do you see inside of that thing? I think in certain situations, it can be a really fun story point. Even in one of the early episodes of *Fringe*, there's a teaser at the end of one of the episodes that is kind of a magic box-y sort of thing where you're like, "What the hell?" I just love that stuff, so that's my own personal interest.'

The trio of Abrams, Kurtzman and Orci met at one of the Comic-Cons to develop ideas for a sci-fi themed show whilst they were also working on the forthcoming *Star Trek* reboot for Paramount. Kurtzman and Orci had just written the summer blockbuster *Transformers* for director Michael Bay and had produced the Shia LaBeouf-led thriller, *Eagle Eye*. Abrams developed the core idea of the show and Peter Roth, the Chief Executive of Warner Bros., Television, heard the pitch for *Fringe* at a dinner meeting in August 2007. Kevin Reilly, the Entertainment Chairman at Fox, worked with Roth to bring the next Abrams project to the network. Given the success of Abrams's previous projects, Warner Bros. Television and Fox Television Network were desperate to have Abrams on board. Jeff Pinkner had previously worked with Abrams on *Alias* and *Lost* and was brought in by Fox to act as the executive producer of *Fringe*. Pinkner's interest was piqued by the show's concept after being informed about it during a visit to the set of *Star Trek*, where Abrams was informally developing it on set with Orci and Kurtzman.

Abrams told *The A. V. Club*'s Noel Murray about his feelings when a TV show of his is about to premiere: 'Well, it's a cocktail of excited for people to see it, terror that no one will watch it, and relief that something I've been working on for so long will finally be out there. Oh, and panic that I can't make more of the little changes we've been making all along. All the times I've been lucky enough to be a part of a show that's actually gotten on the air, it's always that same mixture of excitement and utter fear. Which is kind of what I hope people will feel when they watch *Fringe*.'

As previously mentioned Abrams is a dedicated fan of Rod Serling, creator of *The Twilight Zone*, which originally ran on CBS from 1959 to 1964 and was later revived on TV and adapted to a film. Serling took outlandish ideas and made them seem plausible and with *Fringe*, Abrams endeavoured to do something similar. Serling's other work included the cult TV series *Night Gallery* and the classic dystopian film *Planet of the Apes*, which he co-wrote with Michael Wilson; adapted from the 1963 French novel *La Planète des Singes* by Pierre Boulle. Abrams has always admired the way Serling could drift from TV to film and make equally powerful productions regardless of the size of the screen and budgets.

'I think we all grew up just voraciously devouring television and movies and to be able to spend a day going from movie to movie to movie in a multiplex was like the best day you could possibly have in your life,' Orci told Sheila Roberts of *Movies Online*. 'When you're graced enough to have people allow you to do it, it's like walk into Toys R Us and pick one. It's impossible. You want everything. We all thrive off of the energy I think from each other and the idea of getting to tell lots and lots of stories. It's just fun. It's just what we love to do.'

Abrams drew influences from *The X-Files*, *The Twilight Zone* and *Altered States* as well as the writings of Michael Crichton and the films of David Cronenberg. The creators envisaged *Fringe* to have the procedural techniques of *Law & Order* with the cult appeal of *Lost* and the serialised story style of *Alias*.

*Fringe* is about members of a Federal Bureau of Investigation

'Fringe Division' based in Boston, Massachusetts under the supervision of Homeland Security. The story concerns a team consisting of Olivia Dunham (Anna Tory) – again as with *Alias* a strong female lead, though of a different type – Peter Bishop (Joshua Jackson) and Walter Bishop (John Noble), as they investigate fringe sciences that are all related to a parallel universe. The cast and crew filmed the $10 million pilot in Toronto and later moved to New York and Vancouver where they replicated the film sets. The producers recruited production designer Carol Spier who had worked on a number of David Cronenberg films. The late Leonard Nimoy, famous for playing Spock in the original *Star Trek*, appeared in the first season's finale as Dr William Bell. Nimoy's role recurred in later seasons.

The opening of *Fringe* sees an airplane in trouble, much like the pilot episode of *Lost* but the similarities ended there and Abrams wasn't concerned about it, anyway. He felt the plane in *Fringe* was an appropriate opener. The pilot episode was watched by 13.7 million viewers, and though the first season received only modest reviews from TV critics, as the story developed the show acquired a steady fan base and more positive reviews. The story for the season one finale, 'There's More Than One Of Everything', was written by Bryan Burk with Akiva Goldsman, script by Jeff Pinkner and J.H. Wyman.

Of season one, Micah Towery wrote in *Slant Magazine*: '*Fringe* attempts something similar [to *Lost*] (with an opening scene involving a plane, no less) but can't quite match the primal thrill of vehicular destruction.'

'You can see where it's going, and assuming Abrams doesn't let it get lost in its conspiracy, it should be fun to ride along,' wrote Robert Bianco in *USA Today*.

The creators made some adjustments along the way but the story arc they envisaged at the start of the first series played out nicely. They included many surprises along the way and were excited about how it would develop and what the fan reaction would be. Abrams is a sucker for stand-alone episodes inspired by Rod Serling's *The Twilight Zone* and always saw *Fringe* as a similar sort of production. However, as the series progressed and the parallel universe thread came into play the writers found it increasingly difficult to keep to stand-alone episodes. With *Fringe*, the writers wanted to be scary, funny and exciting and for the most part they succeeded throughout the five seasons. Latter seasons became a vast improvement on the initial one. The fifth and final season was shortened to just thirteen episodes and as a whole five-season creation, *Fringe* is positively reviewed.

Mike Hale reviewed the final season's opener in *The New York Times*: 'On the evidence of Friday's season opener, *Fringe* will continue to be the best show of its kind since *The X-Files* at the grace notes, intimate or humorous instances like Olivia's Crate & Barrel moment (which won't be further spoiled here). When you get the small things right, it's less crucial that your universes and time shifts exactly line up.'

*Fringe* did not achieve the global mainstream appeal of *The X-Files* but it did fill a gap in the TV schedules for such a concept and has since become a firm cult favourite amongst genre fans.

'I feel like it's a show that got to play out as it should have, which is a very rare thing, especially for a show that had middling ratings,' Abrams said to Abbie Bernstein of *Assignment X* about saying goodbye to the show. 'I think for the network to keep the show on is a testament to their wonderful commitment to a show that they actually loved, and I will never forget that. It's a very rare thing.'

Riding high after *Mission: Impossible III*, *Cloverfield* and *Alias*, *Lost* and *Fringe*, Abrams was set for even more mainstream success. The universe was his oyster.

CHAPTER 7

# TO BOLDLY GO...

'You want there to be some kind of portal between reality and fiction.'

**J.J. Abrams, *The Guardian*, 2009**

A major coup for Abrams and for Paramount came in 2009 with the release of *Star Trek*, which he directed and also produced with his *Lost* co-creator Damon Lindelof.

Abrams's *Star Trek* is the eleventh film in the *Star Trek* franchise and a reboot of the original series featuring such famous characters as Captain Kirk, Spock and Scotty. The basic premise is that Kirk, Spock and their crew aboard the USS *Enterprise* tackle the villain Nero; a Romulan from their future who threatens to destroy the United Federation of Planets. The story takes place in an alternate reality and features the original Spock as played by Leonard Nimoy. This clever technique freed the new series from the storylines of the original series, thus opening up the possibility of a whole new fan base.

'And I said to him [Nimoy] you know, here is the thing; I want to talk to you, but I don't know how to talk to you about this, because you are Spock, so I don't care what your autobiography says,' Abrams said at a press conference Q&A as quoted on *Salty Popcorn*. 'And he literally grabbed my shirt and he is like: "no no no tell me tell me tell me" and I realise he is an actor. He is a guy who loves collaboration, wants to know every thought, has an opinion; which is why he is good. But it was this thing of desensitizing myself of the aura of him and just focusing on the actuality of this gentleman who is not only an amazing actor but the definition of grace and kindness and thoughtfulness. He was amazing.'

*Star Trek* was created in 1966 by Gene Roddenberry, a former LA police officer. Optimistic and hopeful about humanity's future, it was cancelled after three seasons, thus bringing an abrupt end to the proposed five-year mission of the USS *Enterprise* and her crew. Five years after the series initially aired, President John F. Kennedy announced 'a new American enterprise' in space and in 1969 Neil Armstrong, an American, became the first man on the moon; getting there before the Russians, though it was the Russians who had won the space race when Yuri Gagarin orbited the Earth on 12 April 1961.

The *Star Trek* franchise both on TV (the 1960s live action series and the animated twenty-two-episode series that ran from 1973 to 1974, originally divided into two seasons) and on the big screen had effectively ended after the lukewarm response to the *Star Trek: Enterprise* TV series, which was eventually cancelled by CBS in 2005, and the failure of the big screen film *Star Trek: Nemesis* (2002). It was former Paramount president Gail Berman who convinced CBS to produce a new feature film and thus relaunch the franchise. They needed a director to open up a new fan base; previous films had lost the audience with dodgy scripts and feeble storylines. Paramount needed a director with vision, someone who could bring together modern resources and technology to create a bold version of *Star Trek* not seen before.

Viacom, who owned Paramount Pictures, split from the CBS Corporation in 2006 and Berman convinced CBS chief executive Leslie Moonves to give them close to two years to develop a new *Star Trek* film before CBS, who owned the rights to the original 1960s TV series, developed a new TV series, which would potentially ruin the chances of success of a big screen movie. In return for the development of a new film CBS would keep its share of the merchandising rights, thus giving them potential profits of millions of dollars. However, the fact that the merchandising rights were split between CBS and Paramount created a nightmare for Bad Robot. The deal states that Paramount must license the *Star Trek* characters from CBS Consumer Products for film merchandising.

Berman went straight to Orci and Kurtzman for ideas for the new film and after the completion of *Mission: Impossible III,* Berman asked Abrams to jump on board with producers Damon Lindelof and Bryan Burk.

When Kurtzman and Orci laid out a tentative script, Abrams was only producing, he hadn't signed on as director yet, but the writers' plan was to lure Abrams over to the director's chair by developing ideas with him before penning the finished script. Burk explained to *Collider*'s Steve 'Frosty' Weintraub: 'J.J. sent off an e-mail to myself, Damon, Alex and Bob that said we're doing *Star Trek* shhhh. I think the subject heading was "shhhh." And then it was like we're doing

*Star Trek*, okay? And as you could imagine, we were all like kind of giddy.'

The writers knew *Trek* fans would not mind multiple storylines and time paradoxes because they are common traits in science-fiction films (and indeed are part of the DNA of *Star Trek*) but there were certain aspects and characteristics of the franchise they could not change. Time travel has always been a fundamental and appropriately acknowledged part of *Star Trek*. The difference between *Star Trek* and *Star Wars* is that the former relies on 'science' and a nod toward quantum physics to make the impossible seem possible while *Star Wars* is science fantasy. 'The characters have not changed as characters,' Kurtzman told *Geek Monthly Magazine*'s Anthony Pascale. 'They still have all the personality traits that we know of the original bridge crew. I think the gravest mistake would have been to try and reinvent the characters. That would have made everybody, including ourselves, very unhappy. It would have felt like violating sacred ground. This was a way to stay true to canon, and to take the stories in a new direction.'

Abrams, Orci and Kurtzman drew inspiration from the *Star Trek* novels as they believed some of the books had merit and would provide fantastic source material. Titles such as *Spock Must Die!* by the renowned science-fiction author James Blish, *Planet of Judgment* and *World Without End* by Joe Haldeman and *Prime Directive* by Judith and Garfield Reeves Stevens are considered to be the epitome of *Star Trek* fan fiction.

Abrams isn't logical, Spock-like you might say, when he approaches a project; it's more like a gut feeling. He doesn't think too much about stuff from the outside when he follows something that interests him. His fear is that he would become too self-aware and thus potentially ruin the project. After reading the script for *Star Trek* he knew that he'd be jealous of whoever would direct it if he turned it down.

'We had a range of relationships with *Star Trek*,' Abrams explained to Sheila Roberts of *Movies Online*, 'and the key was to find a story that we all embraced, again knowing that *Star Trek* inherently was an optimistic story. It told [of] a future that was about collaboration, about survival, about working together across cultural, political, racial lines and spec-ial [species] lines and the idea that we wanted to maintain that spoke to the tone of the movie, which is to say that there were many films in recent years, many of which we have all loved, that have depicted a very dark, dismal, cynical, grim future; and that's not what Roddenberry created and that's not what we were interested in doing and the idea to go back to Kirk and Spock and tell their origins story, create an emotional way in, which would give people like myself a way to love these characters, was an exciting one, and to tell a story that was ultimately optimistic with a big heart. It felt like the movies we loved as kids, and that was one of the things that was the most exciting to work on.'

Some of the later big-screen *Star Trek* adventures lost the sense of fun and humour that was so apparent in some of the original series episodes, notably 'The Trouble with Tribbles', the forty-fourth episode, in which the *Enterprise* is overrun by fluffy, trilling, pink aliens. Humour was something Abrams and his writers wanted to reintroduce to the 2009 film. Kirk, especially, is very funny in the film, displaying all the chauvinistic and cocky attributes of a rock star, while the interplay between McCoy and Spock is often both touching and hilarious.

The look of the film harked back to the original series with lots of primary colours, not just of the uniforms but also the aliens and planets, too. *Star Trek* creates a colourful world which represents its optimism, however naive it may be. Abrams's vision for *Star Trek* would look retro, with miniskirts and tight clothes that looked like they were bought in Carnaby Street in 1960s Swinging London.

The world is a far more cynical place now – we've been into space and to the moon and the space race is more or less over. Communism has (mostly) fallen and we live in a world of social media, corporate corruption and artificial intelligence. *Star Trek* embodies the belief that the human race can go to the stars and into the vastness of space, and as clichéd or trite as it sounds, it is, nevertheless, an exciting prospect. *Star Trek* invites us to believe that a future in the stars is possible. It is the opposite of the sort of future illustrated in, say, *Blade Runner* or *Alien*.

'I remember going to see the first *Star Trek* film with my father, who was a TV/movie producer and he had an office at Paramount,' Abrams said to one interviewer at *Salty Popcorn*. 'He took me to the screening of Robert Wise's film on the lot and I will never forget that, and I actually might even still have the cards that they gave out with the, you know, credits on it, but I remember that great sequence when Kirk is for the first time being taken onto the *Enterprise*, and it was the first time that the *Enterprise* felt real to me; when I saw that and that had a huge impact. And that sequence is five minutes long in the movie; it's a very long sequence but you get to look at that ship, and it is gorgeous and it was shot beautifully so you know in the scene of our film when Kirk is going over to the *Enterprise* I wanted to have a slight hint of you know, that feeling, I wanted to sort of nod to that.'

Abrams was not a *Star Trek* fan per se and had not even seen *Star Trek: Nemesis* because he felt it was disconnected from the original series – he believed *Star Trek* was about Kirk and Spock, which is what he wanted for the reboot. Abrams had never really understood the appeal of the *Star Trek* TV show. It was a little boring to him, though some of his friends enjoyed it. He could never relate to any of the characters – he didn't get the charm of Kirk, or the logic of Spock or the grumpy humour of McCoy and so on, so he let it pass him by.

'I didn't watch the series at all,' Burk admitted to *Collider*'s Steve 'Frosty' Weintraub. 'J.J. references me always at the other end of the spectrum as the dumb guy. Okay? Who's never seen...I didn't see any of them, but there was a reason why I never watched it and we grew up on all the same things which were *Twilight Zone* and all those shows. And I never watched it because I remember vividly tuning in to the show and it would come on and I wouldn't know who these people were and they were just like talking and they were all standing on a bridge and I'd be like "I don't know what the hell's going on."'

Kurtzman, Orci, Lindelof, Burk and Abrams each had different roles in the making of the film, though they each created their own version and merged those ideas to make one unified script. They have good banter and a taut friendship but with *Star Trek* they came to the writers' room with different ideas and approaches. Orci and Lindelof knew the *Star Trek* universe inside out but Abrams and Burk were not fans, so they became the mouthpieces for the non-*Star Trek* fans out there, which made it possible to create a film that appealed to everyone. Their aim was to appease the diehard fans yet make it less intimidating and cool enough for new, perhaps more reluctant, fans. Comic book movies were hugely popular in the 2010s and have been since *Spider-Man* and *X-Men* were released in the early 2000s. Before those films comic book movies were not great successes bar the odd exception, such as Richard Donner's *Superman* in 1978 and Tim Burton's *Batman* in 1989. *Howard the Duck* (produced by George Lucas) hardly raked in the mega bucks. The most successful and appealing comic-book movies in recent times have been new stories that don't follow the originals too closely. With *Star Trek* Abrams and cohorts wanted to make something similar and open the franchise up to audiences who weren't necessarily previously fans of *Star Trek*.

What Abrams and the writers wanted to bring to *Star Trek* was that watching the film would be like watching *Star Wars* back in 1977. Fans who saw the original movie remember to this day going to the cinema, sitting down and watching a giant spectacle unfold in front of their eyes. It was a significant event, a performance. The audience clapped and cheered after the film's climax. *Star Trek* never had that kind of reaction despite its international and vehemently loyal fan base. It was one reason why they decided to explore the origins of Kirk and Spock, as this would invite new fans into the fold.

Despite its science-fiction and fantasy setting Abrams wanted to make the movie seem as real as possible. He wanted to embody the hope and dreams of the original series – swimming against the tide of twenty-first century cynicism. Even though Abrams is not a *Star Trek* fan (he didn't even know Spock was half human!) he did his research and there are still plenty of nods to the original series to please fans. Though Abrams wanted to put his own stamp on the film.

'I will say that I couldn't have done that because I didn't really know those things,' he told *The Sci Fi Show*. 'But luckily the writers do and Bob Orci particularly. I would say he's insane about *Star Trek*. He knows everything, like the arcane details you cannot believe he knows, without having to reference and look up stuff. Every once in a while there's something he's like, "I dunno" and I'm like, "what?" He knows everything. So he's the guy. And the other writers in fairness as well really do know what are the things, the characters, the references to ships and like the Section 31 reference. [A kind of Black Ops 'unofficial' organisation that can bend the rules to defend the Earth or the Federation.] I wouldn't have known Section 31 but they of course did. So there are things that you don't need to know. My favourite movies reference things outside the purview of the film itself and it expands the world and makes it feel like it exists in a universe. Certainly this movie does that as well.'

Regardless of whether Abrams was a *Star Trek* fan or not, he was going to make a film of high action and adventure with romance and comedy. Some *Trek* fans were appalled that he wasn't a fan of the original series.

'Sometimes the truth can sound like manipulation,' he told Matt Bochenski of *Little White Lies* magazine. 'I've taken a lot of flack for the simple fact that I didn't grow up a *Trek* fan, and certainly I don't think that marketing sell is necessarily the smartest thing everywhere. It would have been far easier not to say that and not to talk about it. But I gotta say I think that whatever it is, whether it's something as trivial as entertainment or as important as politics, I think when you speak the truth, people feel it and they know it. This movie is one that, for better or worse, was directed by someone who did not grow up a fan of *Star Trek*, didn't quite get it and always felt that there was a more exciting and thrilling and emotional story to be told.'

The idea of having a director who didn't know what 'T' in James T[iberius] Kirk stood for appalled *Trek* fans. It had been seven years since the previous *Star Trek* film – *Trek* fans wanted a fan at the helm.

'Here's the thing: it definitely put some fans off, and annoyed them. I think they think it's me saying, "I'm better than you,"' he explained to Andrew Pulver of *The Guardian* in 2013. 'But I'm not saying that at all. I am saying that I do not think I was as smart and sophisticated as my friends who loved the show. So I didn't get it, it doesn't mean I'm judging anyone. I have come to love it working on it, but it would be disingenuous of me to say I was a *Trek* fan. I would rather be honest, and hopefully those fans who see what we've done will say: "I'm glad the movies have been made and, if anyone cares at all, he's come to love the thing I loved for so long. Better late than never."'

Though Abrams has yet to make a romantic comedy or a drama he believes that *Star Trek* is as close to that sort of film as he's likely to get at the moment. It's not an obvious romantic comedy and it's not marketed in that fashion but it does have both romance and comedy.

His main focus of the film would be to explore the idea of

the Prime Directive, which forbids Starfleet from interfering in the growth of 'primitive' worlds. The aim of Starfleet is to gain knowledge from other cultures.

Abrams finally accepted Paramount's offer to direct the new *Star Trek* film on 23 February 2007, after initially being on board solely as the show's producer to help out his buddies Orci, Kurtzman and Lindelof. Paramount gave Abrams a budget of $140 million, which was a huge gamble for the studio because the franchise's last film earned less than half that. By October 2007 a script had been finalised but a couple of weeks before they were due to start shooting Abrams wanted a whole new action scene – which would add millions of dollars more to the budget – and the writers' strike was only days away, which meant Kurtzman and Orci had a limited window of opportunity to rewrite the script.

*Star Trek* stars Chris Pine as James T. Kirk, Zachary Quinto as Spock, Karl Urban as Dr Leonard 'Bones' McCoy, Zoe Saldana as Nyota Uhura, John Cho as Kikaru Sulu, Anton Yelchin as Pavel Chekov and Simon Pegg as Montgomery 'Scotty' Scott, with Leonard Nimoy as Spock Prime and Eric Bana as Nero. Pegg, a science-fiction and fantasy fan, could not believe he was sharing scenes with Leonard Nimoy. 'I was just blown away by Simon's sense of humour – but also by his acting skills,' Abrams told *The Guardian*'s Craig McClean. 'He wasn't just funny. He was also surprisingly emotional and convincing. I remember thinking, "holy shit, this guy can probably do anything."'

Abrams and Burk were not the only non-*Star Trek* fans; Chris Pine wasn't a Trekkie (or rather Trekker, to be precise), either. 'I wasn't a fan of *Star Trek*,' he said to *Esquire*'s Sanjiv

Bhattacharya. 'It didn't excite me. All I wanted at that time was a part that I really connected to and when my agent said *Star Trek*, I said, "No! Have you not been hearing anything I've said? *Star Trek* is the furthest thing from what I want to do."'

Pine only turned up to the audition to meet J.J. Abrams and to make a business contact. He even made it clear that he didn't want the part. He took a week to decide if he wanted the role. Ultimately the size, scale and challenge of the film and its history were things that intrigued him more than *White Jazz*, the now defunct movie adaption of James Ellroy's classic crime novel. George Clooney had originally been supposed to appear in *White Jazz*, but had dropped out over scheduling conflicts, at which point Pine had stepped in to replace him. However, the offer of *Star Trek*, and the re-invention of such a major franchise, was too alluring for Pine, and he too eventually left *White Jazz* for the Captain's seat.

Interestingly, Matt Damon was in Abrams's mind for a major role in the film, but not as Kirk. 'I went to Damon for the role of Kirk's father,' Abrams told MTV's Josh Horowitz, 'and he declined in the most gracious and understandable and logical of reasons. We lucked out with Chris Hemsworth, and he did a great job. Maybe it would have been distracting to have someone as massively famous as Matt Damon in that role...The decision was made very early on to have actors who were not necessarily the most famous but the most right for the role.'

Rachel Nichols, star of the recent hit science-fiction series *Continuum*, also had a small part on *Star Trek* as Orion 'Green Girl' Gaila. She'd originally cast for *Lost* but didn't get the part and she also screen-tested for *Mission: Impossible III* but she didn't get that either. Eventually, she was cast in the fifth season of *Alias* in 2005. She finally made it into an Abrams movie with *Star Trek*. 'J.J. always surrounds himself with good people and I've always believed that attitude on set trickles down from the top,' she told *SciFiNow* magazine. 'J.J. is kind and loyal and warm and welcoming and all of his sets are like that, so shooting *Star Trek* was one of those jobs where although the technical parts of it were kind of sticky – five or six hours of hair and make-up with the full body was like, "Oh my god, I've got to be up at 3.45 in the morning" – it's funny and jokey and there's always laughter and there's always a thank you. J.J. will thank people...Everybody just loves him and I really like it when people of that kind of nature see the success that he has.'

When Kurtzman and Orci spoke to Paramount they pitched the idea of two movies in one – they would continue the original storylines by using time travel but also create a new storyline to bring *Star Trek* up-to-date for a new audience. A revised timeline and the concept of time travel gave them the freedom to do as they pleased and thus the opportunity to bring in the original Spock.

There were some criticisms of the story: how could Kirk end up on the same planet as Spock? Abrams argued that the story is about fate and friendship and that it was always Kirk and Spock who drove the original show. 'In the scene, Spock explains that [the encounter of Kirk and Spock Prime] is a result of the universe trying to restore balance after the time line is changed,' Abrams explained to John Scott Lewinski of *Wired* magazine. 'They acknowledged the coincidence as a function of the universe to heal itself.'

Kirk and Spock have a tough love for each other; like Holmes and Watson in the original Conan Doyle *Sherlock Holmes* stories, they are companions who love each other but who exasperate each other. It's a deep friendship. It is something that Pine and Quinto inherited from Shatner and McCoy of the 1960s series. 'I always thought about it more like it was the dialectic of a human being,' Pine said to Shana Naomi Krochmal of *Out* magazine. 'One couldn't be more logic and reason – that's his genetic coding. And the other is more impulsive, following his passion, his fists. That was how it was a functional relationship. You have Spock as the cold reason, you had the passion of Jim Kirk, and then you had the ironic sarcasm of McCoy, which gave the whole thing levity. That dynamic was beautiful.'

However, the casting left one actor more than a little peeved. Mr William Shatner, the legendary actor who played Kirk in the three original series, voiced Kirk in the animated series, played Kirk in the original six movies and dodgy 1994 *Star Trek Generations* crossover movie with the cast of *The Next Generation* and Kirk, Scotty and Chekov from the original series, and the author of some *Trek* novels, was put out that Abrams hadn't cast him. Shatner was James Tiberius Kirk in the eyes of every *Trek* fan. So where the hell was he? Abrams's aim, however, was not to make a *Trek* film aimed at the Trekker but to direct it at science-fiction fans in general, even if it meant pissing off some people.

The first two meetings Abrams and the writers had were separately with William Shatner and Leonard Nimoy, respectively. They agreed to take part and the writers began working on the story. 'At the time we desperately wanted to find a place for Shatner to be in the movie,' Burk explained to *Collider*'s Steve 'Frosty' Weintraub. 'We didn't know how we were going to do it. And in fact there was, I think, scenes in it but they felt like what they were, which were like cameos and weird and they just didn't work. But the idea that you're sitting in a room and you're pitching Kirk/Kirk and Spock/Spock stories … it was so out of body and weird and crazy … Alex and Bob would be going through the story and they'd be like, so Spock, you, would be … and it was just crazy. It was just like really, really weird… And by then I started seeing the series and catching up and whatever so I suddenly began getting into *Star Trek*, so it was all very out of body and weird; particularly you suddenly realise you're working on something that was so iconic in your childhood, even for me. I remember it all and the idea that now you're being allowed to make it is very crazy.'

To cast any other original cast member except Nimoy, it was decided, would have been overkill. Nimoy was a link to the past, as was Majel Roddenberry, widow of *Star Trek*'s creator.

'We were very lucky to have Majel come and do the voice for the Starfleet computer, which she had done in the series and films,' Abrams told *Movies Online*'s Sheila Roberts. 'She came to the set one day when we were shooting on the Nerada and she was just lovely. She was elegant and funny and supportive. It's that crazy thing, we were working with Nimoy so we knew we had someone who had been there and was part of it. Walter Koenig visited the set and that was great. Nichelle [Nichols, Lieutenant Uhura] visited the set. We'd had breakfast with George Takei [Lieutenant Sulu]. But to have Majel come, it was a different kind of thing because she was part of the behind the scenes of it as well as being on camera and to have her say to us that this is it. Basically, she said that Gene would have approved of what we were doing and that meant more than I can say. We always knew we were dedicating the movie to Gene Roddenberry because we never would have obviously been doing any of this if it weren't for him. But sadly, when Majel passed away, we added her name to the card at the end.'

Filming commenced on 7 November 2007 and ended on 27 March 2008, and took place in various locations in California and Utah.

'After I got [the part] and then talking to J.J., the nerves kind of slowly built, because as an actor, and as someone who wants to make a living doing what he loves doing, I was happy to get the part, and that lasts for about fifteen minutes, and you call everyone you know and make plans to move out of your parents' house,' Pine admitted to Josh Horowitz of MTV. 'And then the reality of the situation sets in. Not only is it a tremendous amount of responsibility because of all the money involved, but it's also a franchise that's beloved and it's [the original Kirk] William Shatner to boot. After being scared shitless, I let it go. The fact that we could be eviscerated or succeed was actually liberating.'

Paramount announced in February 2008 that they were moving the release date from 25 December 2008 to 8 May 2009 because they felt more people would see a film in the summer rather than the winter. The final stages of production ended in late 2008, which gave writer Alan Dean Foster time to write the novelization in time for the film's official release.

Composer Michael Giacchino spoke to *Geek Nation*'s Ben

Pearson about the pressures of making a *Star Trek* soundtrack following such revered film composers as Jerry Goldsmith and James Horner: 'The only pressure I feel is the pressure I put on myself. It's not from anyone outside of this. If you think about *Mission: Impossible*, I love that theme so much and I love Lalo Schifrin and his music, so it was more about, "I don't want to disappoint Lalo." Or even with *Star Trek*, I don't want to disappoint the fans, but I can't also repeat what was already done. So there are those kinds of feelings you kind of go with, but in the end you just have to go with, "what are we making here? What should our movie sound like?" and you have to sort of let go of those things.'

'We have amazing sound people working with us on everything,' Bryan Burk told Sheila Roberts of *Movies Online*. 'Mark Stoeckinger was our sound designer and then there was a window at the end of the year where we wanted to have a lot of these very iconic sounds that were obviously in the original series and Ben Burtt, who is arguably one of the fathers of sound design with *Star Wars* and everything else, happened to be available. We were able to get him and to say we're sycophants of his is an understatement. Just working with him and then working with Andy Nelson and Anna [Behlmer], we had these incredible mixers and we spent a lot of time, more time than usual actually, doing the mixes and going back in and really kind of making sure that there was always something present – be it the sound effects or the music – and then all the silence. That all came out of J.J. perpetually liking the idea of really loud, then silent, then really loud, then silent. We referenced a lot like *The Exorcist*, which for me had incredible sound design. You're terrified watching that movie. You could be terrified covering your eyes just because it's loud, soft, loud, soft. It's kind of a fun process that at the end of making the movie we just spent a little extra time.'

Robert Orci, Alex Kurtzman and Damon Lindelof hosted a surprise public screening of the film on 6 April 2009 at the Alamo Drafthouse in Austin, Texas. Ingeniously, the screening was advertised as *Star Trek II: The Wrath of Khan* (the 1982 movie) with a ten-minute preview of the new film; but some visual effects kicked in, making the screen look as though it was melting and Leonard Nimoy appeared with the three producers/writers asking the audience if they'd rather see the new film instead. Hell yeah, they exclaimed! Paramount promoted the film heavily and premiered the film in various cities around the world including Austin, Texas; Sydney, Australia and Calgary, Alberta.

Paramount had a lot riding on the rebirth of the franchise: most of the profits from the *Transformers* movie went to DreamWorks and the *Mission: Impossible* franchise stalled with Tom Cruise's infamous jump for joy declaring his love for Katie Holmes on *The Oprah Winfrey Show* in 2005.

'In terms of Tom's publicity,' Abrams said to *IGN*'s Stax on the subject, 'I am sure you can find evidence that any publicity is good publicity, and also find evidence equally valid that having him go on *Oprah* is not a good thing for him.'

Abrams with Orci and Kurtzman wanted to learn from the mistakes of the first big screen *Star Trek* adventure, 1979's *The Motion Picture*, which is generally considered to be one of, if not the, weakest of the big-screen *Trek* adventures. It is generally thought by fans that the odd numbered films are the weakest, making the far superior second film, *The Wrath of Khan*, the starting point for many fans, and continuing with the fourth film, *The Voyage Home*. *The Motion Picture* was directed by Robert Wise, director of such classics as *The Haunting* and *The Day the Earth Stood Still*, yet despite the stunning visuals by the legendary Douglas Trumbull, *The Motion Picture* failed to properly ignite with a weak script and over reliance on special effects while *The Wrath of Khan* has a much better story, villain, pacing and action scenes. The director of *The Wrath of Khan*, Nicholas Meyer, also scripted and directed the sixth film, *The Undiscovered Country*, which, again, reignited interest in the series after the failure of the fifth film, *The Final Frontier*; directed by none other than James T. Kirk himself, William Shatner. Abrams needed to make a film as memorable as the best *Star Trek* cinema outings.

Abrams's version of *Star Trek* is a character study – it's all about the crew. Abrams defied those sceptical fans who felt he was the wrong man for the job – he brought together a grand vision of the *Star Trek* universe and created a stunning spectacle.

What had Abrams learned during the making of not one but eventually two big-screen *Trek* films? 'The fact is those are wonderful characters and incredible relationships, and the funny thing is that *Star Trek* always felt a little bit sort of phony and sort of self-serious and stuff,' he said to Tavis Smiley of PBS, 'I came to appreciate it so much more, the intelligence of the debates, the political ramifications of – what Roddenberry was doing when he created *Star Trek* was obviously such a comment on where we were as a country at the time. The idea of people working together, the unity of people from various countries, different races, all working together, that never being an issue between them at all, it's just us, as humans, working together, it's sort of an undeniably beautiful thing. Stuff that was far more impactful and important that I was just not looking at suddenly became the tenets of why this thing was so great. So I've become, like, an evangelist about *Star Trek*, whereas as a kid, I was always like, "Ah." It just didn't click with me, and now I kind of see why my friends were such fans.'

With such a young and good-looking cast Abrams and his actors had made *Star Trek* cool and who knows, maybe younger fans would pay a visit to the original series? 'You know, making a film knowing there were so many fans out there was nerve-racking,' Pine admitted to MTV's Josh Horowitz. 'I was behind the camera. Chris, Zach [Quinto], Zoe [Saldana], John [Cho], Simon [Pegg], Karl [Urban] – everyone in front of the camera – they were the ones literally putting themselves out there and asking for it. The fact that we were accepted and helped by Mr Nimoy building that bridge between what was and what is now, it was incredibly gratifying to see it was well-received.'

Reviews of the film were very positive and box-office success was strong as it grossed over $300 million worldwide, which is a staggering amount of money for a *Star Trek* film, especially in the 2010s.

'…I would say I was surprised at how emotional it turned out,' Orci said to *Geek Monthly* magazine's Anthony Pascale of the film. 'Especially for something that is considered a big action and sci-fi movie, emotion is the last word that comes to mind, but it really is emotional. Because again it was important to make it about the characters and the people, not just make it about spectacle.'

Some felt the film suffered because of the lens flare, which is an enormous amount of light directed at the camera, sometimes causing headaches and feelings of dizziness for viewers. Simon Pegg came rushing to Abrams's defence in an interview with Steve 'Frosty' Weintraub of *Collider*: 'It's become a sort of a communal stick to have a crack at J.J. with, mostly by people who didn't know what the fuck lens flare was, until someone started sneering the term all over their blog. It demonstrates J.J.'s supreme talent as a filmmaker that the main means of knocking him is to magnify a throw-away artistic choice, into some sort of hilarious failing. Lens flare is essentially an anomaly caused by light hitting the lens and creating refracted shapes. Because it draws attention to the fact that we are looking at a filmed event, it actually creates a subliminal sense of documentary realism and makes the moment more vital and immediate. In the same way Spielberg spattered his shots with bloody seawater in *Saving Private Ryan*, J.J. suggests that the moment we are in is so real and alive, there just isn't time to frame out all the light and activity.'

The lens flare was not the only complaint some people had. Levar Burton who played Geordi La Forge in *Star Trek: The Next Generation* said it was missing Gene Roddenberry's vision and stressed that the new *Star Trek* movies were J.J. Abrams's interpretation of *Star Trek*; no one else's. '[Abrams's *Star Trek*] was a great movie,' he told the *Toronto Sun*'s Jim Slotek, 'and he brought a whole new generation to *Trek*. But I'm a little disquieted by things I hear coming out of his camp, things like he would like to be remembered as the only *Trek* – which would discount everything before he got there. There's "breaking the canon," which he did [by reinventing

*Star Trek*'s timeline]. But there's also honouring the canon. And to pretend to be the only one is really egocentric and immature. I just came from a conference in San Francisco with Advanced Micro Devices, and they're working on technology towards building a holodeck. That was *Next Generation*. And that's part of what *Star Trek* has brought to the culture. So when J.J. Abrams says, "There should be no *Star Trek* except the one I make," I call "bulls–, J.J."'

On the critical front, the film did rather well. Peter Bradshaw raved over it in his five-star review in *The Guardian*: 'Unlike George Lucas's massively encumbered and obese *Star Wars* prequel-trilogy, this new *Star Trek* is fast-moving, funny, exciting warp-speed entertainment and, heaven help me, even quite moving – the kind of film that shows that, like it or not, commercial cinema can still deliver a sledgehammer punch. It sure didn't feel like a trek to me.'

'…Complaints of insufficiently evil interior decorating hardly put much of a dent in Abrams's achievement,' wrote Tim Robey in *The Daily Telegraph*. 'This is a grand success – perhaps a new populist benchmark in what to do with a flagging franchise, and a witty, light-on-its-feet prequel which makes instant toast of *X-Men Origins: Wolverine*. May it live long and prosper, by which we mean, sequels, soon, please.'

Writing in *The New Yorker* Anthony Lane said of Abrams, as mentioned in Chapter One: 'He is the perfect purveyor of fictions to a generation so easily and instinctively jaded that what it craves, above all, is a storyteller who – with or without artistic personality, and regardless of any urge to provoke our thoughts or trouble our easy dreams – will never jade. Hence the demeanour of the new film.'

In the *Huffington Post*, Scott Mendelson wrote: 'J.J. Abrams' ambitious *Star Trek* reboot desperately tries to have it both ways. Not confident enough to choose its path, it straddles between affectionately campy homage and its own franchise. Like Bryan Singer's *Superman Returns*, it is too afraid to boldly chart its own destiny, but refusing to be a true extension of the original franchise. While it portends to separate itself from the *Star Trek* mythology that inspired it, the picture completely counts on said mythology for any and all emotional impact.'

The cast signed on for two more films as part of a planned trilogy. Abrams was incredibly proud of the production and the cast with the job they did. Again, Abrams enjoyed working with non-star actors. It tends to be a case of less ego and more ambition.

'I remember meeting William Shatner and Leonard Nimoy separately and just hearing their stories about what *Star Trek* was like back in the day was wonderful,' Abrams said to *Its Art Mag*. 'The first screening of the movie we had with an audience was the premier at the Sydney Opera House and that was an incredible evening. It was so big that I couldn't tell if they hated the movie or not. I couldn't tell what the reaction was. And I was fairly certain that they didn't like it because it was such a big place and you couldn't hear the audience the way that you can in a normal movie theatre and then when it was over they gave it a two minute standing ovation and it was just this crazy relief of "Oh OK, they didn't hate it." That was really nice.'

*Star Trek* fans, like sci-fi fans in general, are often mocked for being nerds and geeks. 'It can be [hard]' Abrams told Scott Myers of *Playboy*, being a *Trek* fan. 'The key in everything we did was to embrace the spirit with which *Star Trek* was approached in the 1960s. So the design of the props, the locations and certainly the characters themselves couldn't be mockeries or impersonations but had to be as deeply felt as Leonard Nimoy felt and applied to his interpretation of the character in his time. Zachary Quinto, who plays Spock, had to do his own version of that, just as we never wanted Chris Pine to do a Shatner parody. Audiences pick up on that stuff. Not only are we post-*Star Trek* the series and movies, but we're post-*Galaxy Quest*, post-*Saturday Night Live* spoofs. We were coming at this post-*Trek* satire, so we needed to be earnest in the right places and funny in the right places or people would have made fun of us.'

Asked by *The Guardian*'s Katie Puckrik if he was now responsible for making geeks appear cool (thanks also in no small part to the likes of Simon Pegg and the success of the TV show, *The Big Bang Theory*) he replied: 'First of all, the definition of geek has changed. When I started, a geek was an undeniable loser: long-necked, trips over his own feet, a complete outcast. And now geek means someone who likes science-fiction. When I was a kid, it was a huge insult to be a geek. Now it's a point of pride in a weird way. I feel very lucky to be working in a business and to be part of stories that are embraced by people who fit the current definition of geek. And also maybe the occasional athlete.'

By the turn of the 2000s Abrams, much like his hero Steven Spielberg, was becoming a celebrity in his own right. He featured in the 2009 MTV Movie Awards digital short 'Cool Guys Don't Look at Explosions', which starred Andy Samberg and Will Ferrell. The 1980s-style piece saw Abrams play a keyboard solo. Abrams had become the king of Hollywood with billions of dollars in box-office receipts. The days of penning scripts for other filmmakers, including the risible (but successful) *Armageddon*, were long gone.

He served as executive producer and writer of the 2009 TV pilot *Anatomy of Hope*, based on the book *The Anatomy of Hope: How People Prevail in the Face of Illness* by Jerome Groopman about the lives of cancer patients in a hospital. The series was planned to be aired by HBO but they did not pick it up after the pilot. 2009 saw the release of such acclaimed shows as *The Good Wife*, *Lie to Me*, *Castle*, *White Collar* and *Community*. *The Anatomy of Hope* was a failure, sadly, but then again, it wasn't given much of a chance to be a hit.

The *Star Trek* director then went on to produce (with Bryan Burk) the little remembered 2010 film *Morning Glory*. Directed by Roger Mitchell and written by Aline Brosh McKenna, *Morning Glory* is a comedy starring Harrison Ford, Diane Keaton and Rachel McAdams. The story is simple: a young and enthusiastic TV producer named Becky Fuller (played by McAdams) gets hired as an executive producer on the popular long-running morning show *DayBreak* at a once-successful station in NYC. She tries to save the ailing show by using a former news journalist and anchor (played by Ford) but he does not like co-hosting a show that doesn't revolve around hard news stories. The film was released in the US in November 2010 and in early 2011 overseas after delays and was only a modest box office and critical success. It was *Broadcast News*- and *Network*-lite.

'Harrison Ford gives an under-par performance in this

disappointing TV-studio-set romantic comedy,' wrote Peter Bradshaw in *The Guardian*.

Philip French was also not impressed by the film. He wrote in *The Observer*: 'This deeply dislikable comedy of embarrassment, which uses rock music like narrative Polyfilla, stars Rachel McAdams as Becky, an unintentionally unprincipled, motor-mouthed TV producer.'

Abrams continued his endeavours in TV with another misfire: the spy series *Undercovers* was created (and executive-produced by Abrams) and Josh Reims. *Undercovers* just didn't seem as fresh or as vital as the shows that were causing a stir in the 2010 TV season, such as *Boardwalk Empire*, *The Walking Dead*, and *Game of Thrones*. *Undercovers* was cancelled after just one season due to low ratings. It aired from September to December 2010.

'This show does have ongoing stories as well but they are much more personal-based and character-based,' Abrams told Brian Ford Sullivan of *The Futon Critic*. 'But I'm trying to do a show that has a more fun energy and a little more comedic than [*Fringe*]...There won't be any of [the Rambaldi-type mythology, i.e. *Alias*]. I think that there will be, again, something that will give the story a sense of inevitability and yet, you're right, it won't be going into that place of like crazy, mythology heavy stuff.'

The pilot was directed by Abrams, which marked the first time he'd directed a pilot since *Lost* in 2004 and his first time directing a TV episode since one of *The Office* back in 2007. 'I just enjoyed the idea of it,' Abrams said to *The Futon Critic*'s Brian Ford Sullivan on why he chose to direct the pilot. 'I enjoy the script... I enjoyed the chemistry of these two people and it became clear as we were working on it, rather than be sitting on the set every day with someone else directing it, being annoying, I'd rather just take the burden on myself.'

His intention for *Undercovers* was to have more comedy and to make it more personal than his previous foray into the world of spies on TV with *Alias*. 'You know,' Abrams told *The Guardian*'s Andrew Pulver in 2013, 'there was no strategy about my career; no idea to create a resumé of work that said anything in particular. All I went on, really, was my gut feeling about projects. Would it be a challenge, would it be fun, would it be an entertainment that I could believe I could do justice to?'

The press were not convinced.

Mary McNamara wrote in the *LA Times*: 'The writers seem so concerned with ensuring that their characters are preternaturally decent and likable that they go for sunny skies when there should be storm clouds...But Kodjoe and Mbatha-Raw are so energetic and appealing that it's hard to take your eyes off them long enough to worry about such matters, and they both seem up for just about anything.'

In the *New York Post* Linda Stasi said: 'The guy who brought you *Alias*, *Fringe*, and the not-so-successful but interesting *Dollhouse* [sic], so, of course, the expectations are high. No, *Undercovers* isn't as good as those shows, but it is still a lot of fun.'

Abrams spoke about the failure of *Undercovers* to *Buzzy Mag*'s Abbie Bernstein: 'I've got to say, I didn't feel the problem with that show was my being over-extended. I thought the problem with that show was, I made bad choices. I wasn't as respectful of the audience or the characters – I didn't give people anything of substance. And the thing that's fun about fluff is, it needs to be contextualized, it needs to be fun and fluffy within something of meaning. And it was kind of fluff on top of fluff, as opposed to something more substantial. And Josh Reims [who co-created the series with Abrams], who I would work with again, kind of took my lead on that in a big way and I just honestly wrote it into mediocrity. And I feel guilty, because I love the actors, I love the idea of the show, I love the idea of a couple that love each other, but ultimately, if you don't have great conflict, what do you have?'

Rumours floated around that Abrams was going to write and produce an adaptation of Stephen King's *The Dark Tower* series of fantasy novels about a gunslinger called Roland Deschain, but nothing came to fruition.

It's interesting how his hit-and-miss career in TV mirrors Steven Spielberg's, who has also had a topsy-turvy background in TV, with the so-so anthology series *Amazing Stories*, the modestly received *SeaQuest DSV* and the awful *Terra Nova* alongside *Falling Skies* and *Under the Dome*, both of which are quite good. His best known TV work is the outstanding *Band of Brothers*, though the over-Americanised *The Pacific* didn't quite hit the spot. Nevertheless, he's never quite hit all the right buttons in television the way he has in cinema, despite his extensive output on the small screen.

Abrams had been involved with a couple of TV failures but had *Felicity*, *Alias*, *Lost* and *Fringe* to his name at this time and would add even more hit shows to his resumé in future years. However, a major cinematic collaboration was just around the corner that would seem like a childhood fantasy come true. The film would mark Abrams's first collaboration with perhaps the most well-known and successful director in the entire history of cinema. It would be a more personal affair than *Mission: Impossible III* and *Star Trek* and one that would entrance everyone who grew up loving Hollywood popcorn movies in the 1970s and 1980s.

CHAPTER 8

# WORKING WITH HIS HERO

'I have no idea why anything does or doesn't get made.'

**J.J. Abrams, *Slash Film*, 2011**

Abrams's *Super 8*, his homage to Steven Spielberg (who produced it with Bryan Burk) was released in 2011. Abrams wrote, directed and produced.

When Abrams came up with the idea for *Super 8* Spielberg was the first person he called, but he was concerned the collaboration might not happen because he had a film deal with Paramount and Spielberg was with DreamWorks. But Abrams did not want to make the film with anyone else.

'When I called Steven, it was an instinct to work with someone who was a hero of mine since I was a kid, and I had no idea what the movie was,' said Abrams to Katie Puckrik of *The Guardian*. 'All I had was the title, and knew this could be a movie about a group of kids making movies, and he was the one person I knew who had done this the way I had, who could help a movie like that get made. So I called him, and he said yes.'

Abrams and Spielberg held a storytelling meeting and generated the concept, though press reports suggested it was going to be a sequel to *Cloverfield*. Abrams and Spielberg had countless meetings before Abrams started writing the film. Spielberg was both encouraging and critical but always very enthusiastic.

'I had been working on a number of ideas about kids making movies – a kind of junior *Day For Night*,' said Spielberg to *Entertainment Weekly*. 'So we kind of brought our ideas together. We also share a passion for science-fiction, so it was an interesting merger that took place between us. What appealed to me of what J.J. was pitching was that it was an idea that was biographical for both of us.'

*Super 8* was the product of two ideas which Abrams combined, figuring that neither idea was strong enough to generate its own individual film. One idea was about a group of kids in small-town America making their own movie during the 1970s and the other idea was a blockbuster alien movie.

'I have no idea why anything does or doesn't get made,' Abrams said to Peter Sciretta of *SlashFilm*. 'But I feel like there was a kind of movie that I watched when I was younger, which was a movie that had believable characters that made you laugh, that made you comfortable, that then went through something insane and extraordinary … And by the end of the movie you didn't just go through something that made you scared, and laugh, and amazed, but also made you emotional and perhaps even made you cry. And there was something about those movies that were simultaneously moving and also fantastical.'

He continued: 'Those were the kind of movies that I loved.

I'm not saying that you can't never try them at all. But there was a kind of movie that I loved when I was a kid where I would be laughing one minute, crying the next minute, I would be amazed the next, and scared the next. And by the time the movie is over I felt like I had been through this sort of roller coaster of various emotions and it was a wonderful, satisfying thing. The goal of *Super 8* was to try to make a movie that was not just a comedy, not just a horror movie, not just a science-fiction film, not just a love story, not just an emotional family trauma or a weird sort of paranoid thriller, but all of them.'

*Super 8*, though, did not start out as a homage to anything.

'…As I started working on the story, it was clear that this felt like it could be a movie that would live under the Amblin umbrella,' Abrams revealed to *SheKnows*. 'And then, Steven himself said, "This should be an Amblin movie." I don't think an Amblin movie has ever had its title at the beginning of the film. The idea of it being one of those movies was freeing because suddenly I thought, "Oh, that's what this movie is." It is small-town America, in that era, with these people, with these families, and with this otherworldly thing that is happening. There's a little pang of guilt you get when you have kids jump on these BMX bikes. Can you really have kids on bikes? Well, if you're doing a movie in 1979, what are they going to do? That's what they did. They're kids.'

Whether *Super 8* was intended as a homage to Spielberg or not (and it really does feel as though it is), or even if it just ended up that way by circumstance or coincidence there is no doubt that there are similarities between *Super 8* and Spielberg classics *E.T.*, *Close Encounters of the Third Kind* and *Jurassic Park*, and even the Spielberg-produced movie, *The Goonies* with a story by Christopher Columbus (another Spielberg protégé) and directed by Richard Donner. The fun part of making the film for Abrams was actually working with a director who inspired him; a guy who made a bunch of films that Abrams loved growing up in 1970s LA. A guy who happened to be the most famous film director in the world: Steven Spielberg.

In 1979, the year the film is set, Abrams was a kid who was massively influenced by Spielberg, much like the teenage wannabe movie maker in *Dawson's Creek*, the cheesy 1990s TV show that is filled with Spielberg references thanks to its film-fanatic lead character, Dawson Leery. Abrams was trying to create the spirit of those Amblin films; not necessarily recreate the scenes. On set Abrams even had flashbacks to when he was a kid growing up in LA. The books, comics, toys and movie memorabilia reminded him of being a kid and visiting his friends' houses.

'…I know it's about his [Abrams'] childhood,' fellow director Matt Reeves said to *Collider*'s Steve 'Frosty' Weintraub, 'and I shared so much of that time with him. When I saw that movie, in addition to loving the movie, when it got to the end titles and it had that film the kids had made [it was] just so evocative of the films J.J. and I made when we were kids that it blew me away.'

What Abrams did not want was *Super 8* to be a 'lost footage' type of film of the kind that had become increasingly popular in Hollywood, most particularly in the horror genre with films such as *Paranormal Activity*, *REC* and *Quarantine*, popularised after 1999's *The Blair Witch Project*. And obviously not forgetting *Cloverfield*.

'There was no master list of movies that needed to be borrowed from,' he told *SheKnows*, 'but it just felt like these

*Above left*: Abrams's trophy cabinet must be fairly full by now, but the two Emmys he won in 2005 are surely in pride of place.

*Above right*: One of the perks of the job: at the *Mission: Impossible III* premiere with Tom Cruise.

*Below left*: J.J. Abrams (*left*) with some of the cast of *Mission: Impossible III*, including Keri Russell (*second from right*), who he had worked with extensively on *Felicity*.

*Below right*: With Katie McGrath, to whom J.J. has been happily married for almost two decades.

*Left*: Joel Courtney and Riley Griffiths taking direction on the set of Abrams's passion project *Super 8*.

*Right*: On the USS *Enterprise* with (*from left*) Simon Pegg, Zoe Saldana, Chris Pine, Karl Urban, Anton Yelchin and John Cho.

*Left*: A battered Chris Pine in serious conversation with Abrams.

*Left*: Abrams cuts a dramatic figure in front of the bridge of the USS *Enterprise*.

*Right*: The long-time collaborator Alex Kurtzman has worked with Abrams on a wide-ranging number of productions.

*Left*: The *Star Trek* cast reunited for *Star Trek Into Darkness*, along with the excellent *Sherlock* star Benedict Cumberbatch.

*Above*: There's much more to being a Hollywood mogul than just making movies. Abrams worked with First Lady Michelle Obama on Joining Forces, an organisation designed to help America's military families.

*Above*: Bad Robot has been an enormous success since being founded in 1998 by J.J. Abrams and Bryan Burk (*far left*).

*Left*: Abrams appeared with co-author Doug Dorst in New York to discuss their highly unusual and innovative novel *S*.

were the characters and that was the world. So, when they got on their bikes, I felt like it was a celebration, as opposed to something to get over with quickly and be ashamed of, for borrowing heavily from *E.T.* or something.'

Spielberg was enthusiastic about the story from the get-go while Abrams was keen to revisit his youth. 'I have not put my Super-8 films on DVD, because seriously, why do that to The People?' he told Richard Corliss of *Time Entertainment*. 'Most of my first movies were excuses to test things out: primitive visual effects accomplished by backwinding the film and exposing it twice, or testing out makeups on my family and friends, or doing fight scenes or chases. Later I started telling stories with a narrative, though viewers of those films might question that statement.'

Much like Spielberg, Abrams has immersed himself in every aspect of filmmaking and is constantly keeping up-to-date with the latest technologies. He knows how to market a modern-day movie with viral marketing campaigns, merchandising gimmicks and tie-ins, forums and online communities, blogs, websites, spoiler alerts and TV trailers.

What Abrams loves about Spielberg's work is that feeling of wonder and unlimited possibilities. Spielberg could bring anything to life – spaceships in *Close Encounters of the Third Kind* or a lost alien who befriends a boy in *E.T.* or an archaeology teacher who's an adventurer as in *Raiders of the Lost Ark*. With Spielberg films, there is usually an emotive connection between the characters onscreen and the audience. There is humour, depth and warmth in Spielberg's best films and Abrams endeavoured to have such traits in *Super 8*.

'We talked about many ideas to round it out,' said Spielberg to *Entertainment Weekly*. 'One idea I threw onto the table was that these kids would be making a movie, and in the background of the movie they were making, there was a bank robbery or something. The only evidence of this crime [would have been] inadvertently captured by these kids making this innocent movie. But we both threw that out.'

It took a while for Abrams to make the story as personal as he wanted it to be. They came up with all sorts of ideas at first. But he had not yet found an idea that made him, as a film fan, want to see the film. They even thought of bringing in another writer. Abrams remembered an idea he once pitched to Paramount about a train derailment. He was making *Star Trek* at the time and someone told him a story about how the American military had clandestinely removed all the contents of Area 51 to other secret government locations. He then started to ask himself questions: how could they move them without people finding out? What sort of vehicles did they use to move them? Then it clicked – what if they moved all this secret stuff from Area 51 to another location and the train crashed and whatever was inside was discovered? What if it was a monster and the monster escaped? He pitched the idea to Spielberg and they merged their ideas together and suddenly found something incredibly exciting and personal.

It was uncertain whether Abrams was going to direct it or not. Abrams wanted a solid script before he even thought about sitting on the director's chair. However, as soon as the script started to come together Abrams knew that no one but he himself could direct it.

A fan of new actors and faces, Abrams held a talent search to find new child actors for the leading roles. Starring Joel

Courtney, Elle Fanning and Kyle Chandler, the film follows the story of a group of kids who are filming their own Super 8 zombie movie in a small Ohio town in 1979 when a train derails and releases an unknown presence into their town.

'Joel [Courtney] was really impressive,' Abrams enthused to *Time Entertainment*'s Richard Corliss. 'He had never acted professionally before. He lives in Moscow, Idaho. Once a month his family would drive him to an acting school in Seattle, Washington. That's how much he loved the craft and wanted to learn – and it is how he was able to audition [a local casting director reached out to acting teachers]. Of course, like with any actor, you edit out the moments that don't work, but Joel gave the film an abundance of moments that did.'

'There was this one time during the auditioning process where he wanted us to understand about one character,' Courtney told *Screen Rant*'s Roth Cornet, 'and so he pretty much just told us the entire life story of that one character. And he did it in like thirty seconds flat. He described everything about the character – it was so incredible.'

Abrams's level of detail is extraordinary, almost like the notoriously difficult director Stanley Kubrick's, in wanting every minute piece of the film exactly how he envisaged it. However, Abrams gave the child actors a level of freedom which other filmmakers possibly wouldn't allow. Abrams wanted spontaneity and naturalism. This shines through in the relationship between Joel Courtney's character Joe and his love interest, Alice, played by Elle Fanning. Abrams even allowed the actors to write the short film *The Case*, which the characters are making to submit to a film festival. They used improvisation and were inspired by the likes of *Shaun of the*

*Dead* and *Zombieland*. It was a dream come true for a bunch of kids not only to be given the opportunity to star in a major Hollywood production but to make their own little zombie film. Despite the premise of the film, Abrams wanted everything to seem as real as possible so he gave the kids as much freedom as he dared. They injected their own personalities into the film and some of their own influences and it shows in *The Case* as well as *Super 8*.

'It was tough, frankly, finding them because it's not just a binary thing, where you're casting one person,' Abrams confessed to *SheKnows* about casting. 'Even if you found that one person, it's also about how they work with the other people we needed to cast, so part of it was the group. And Elle came in towards the end. We were looking for everyone. Just because she had done some work didn't mean that it was a given. I had met her when she was around on the *War of the Worlds* set, as this little tiny baby sister of Dakota, so even the idea of Elle was like, "What?! She's like one. She's eight inches tall. There's no way!" [*Laughs*] And then, when she came in and had more poise and sophistication than any of us, it was insane. I was like, What?! She can't be twelve. It's impossible. And, it wasn't like she had an attitude about it. She was just wise. The truth is that we saw thousands of kids, for months and months and months. Joel [Courtney] was great and Riley [Griffiths] as well. They were professional people who were young enough to be that age, and then acted that age. They were just those kids.'

The reason why Abrams chose 1979 was because he felt it was the end of an era and the twelve to fourteen age bracket of the group of childhood also represented the end of childhood and how that sense of innocence and naivety is lost. Abrams wanted to catch the kids right on the edge of puberty. Actually at the end of production two of the child actors' voices dropped two octaves! Abrams joked that it was lucky it didn't happen during filming. Elle Fanning is excellent in the film and some critics later pointed out that she has star quality. The idea of making a film set in the noughties with kids with iPhones and laptops making movies with their smart phones and uploading them on YouTube held no interest at all for Abrams. It's not something he could relate to on a personal and emotional level. It was about the era, because in the 1970s kids who made movies were seen as oddballs and outcasts because not every kid had a camera the way every contemporary kid has a phone, and Abrams wanted to recreate that. Making movies as a teenager in the 1970s was a lot of effort because there was only so much film and you had to make choices with limited resources.

*Super 8* references other films and though Abrams did not make Courtney watch those films he felt he had to do some research. 'I had watched (and loved) *E.T.* and *Close Encounters* already,' Courtney admitted to *Screen Rant*'s Roth Cornet, 'but I hadn't watched *Stand by Me* and *The Goonies*, and so I watched those two during production and all of his references made sense, after I watched those two movies. It was really incredible because there's so much Steven Spielberg and J.J. collaboration on this movie. You can see it throughout the entire movie. Like, the group of kids and J.J.'s sci-fi thrown in there – it's like, so apparent.'

Charles Kaznyk, the filmmaker in *Super 8* played by Riley Griffiths, watched Abrams on set to see how he worked –

unbeknownst to Abrams. 'I feel like I was never as confident as the director kid in *Super 8*,' Abrams confessed to *Den of Geek*'s Luke Savage, 'I was sort of more the – I feel like I'm more the other kid, Joe. I was the kid making the movies, but I also was the kid who loved to blow stuff up. And I was never as smart as the kid Preston, or as stupid as Martin. So, I was somewhere in the middle of all of them, I think.'

*Super 8* is self-evidently a tribute to Amblin Entertainment. It would be difficult for a filmmaker of Abrams's generation to make a film about a group of kids that's set in 1979 without being influenced by films either directed, written or produced by Spielberg. Working with Spielberg on a tribute to *ET* et al. and being produced and released by Amblin gave Abrams the freedom to embrace the DNA of the earlier films. It was all about Amblin and Abrams's nostalgic visit to the American pop culture of his youth.

'The plan is not to emulate,' Burk told the *San Diego Reader*'s Matthew Lickona about their intention with *Super 8*, 'it's just that often, you find yourself having overlap when you try to capture the feelings that you had during those movies that you saw, particularly during childhood. There are those great movies that you see, and it's a very singular experience. I can remember where I was sitting in the theatre for certain films. It's a lot of trying to dissect those moments, why they worked. The jumping off point is, "Why do I care about this character?" I'm not looking at it as nostalgia. Or it's only in retrospect that I'm looking at nostalgia. At the time, it's just what's ingrained in everything I think and everything that inspires me.' ('It's only in retrospect that I'm looking at nostalgia' has a neat ring to it.)

*Super 8* shows how subtle Abrams is as a storyteller. With each scene he slowly let slip a vital part of the plot, which engaged the audience and kept them on their toes throughout. It made the story more effective. Abrams was inspired by a deleted scene from *Alien*, directed by Ridley Scott, where Veronica Cartwright's character is about to be attacked. Abrams learned that withholding certain scenes and shots can create an intense film only if the climax is substantial. Abrams found it hard to keep the central story as taut as possible because he had to balance a coming-of-age drama with a monster movie.

Creating the monster for the film was a challenging job because Abrams wanted it to be frightening and intimidating but also emotive, empathetic and sympathetic. It meant creating a monster that had some human characteristics, such as eyes and a mouth.

Abrams told Richard Corliss of *Time Entertainment*: 'Before we were shooting I told our cinematographer, Larry Fong – whom I met at twelve making Super-8 films – that I didn't want the film to look like it was made in 1979, but I wanted it to look the way we *remember* films looking from 1979. That is to say, it needed to be its own thing, with visual and rhythmic motifs that allude to a different era of moviemaking, but made using tools and techniques of today. I sort of wanted to build a bridge between then and now. The story worked the same way: it needed to stand on its own, but with nods to its origins and conventions of the genre. But I never had a checklist of shout-outs [expressions of thanks] that I wanted to make.'

LA-born Larry Fong was a self-taught filmmaker. He had

learned the rigours of filmmaking from an early age by making 8mm movies with cell animation and stop motion during junior high. He later graduated from UCLA with a Bachelor of Arts degree in linguistics and film and photography at Art Centre College of Design in Pasadena. His entrance into professional cinematography began in music videos, commercials, short films and TV episodes before being hired to work on the *Lost* pilot in 2004, which garnered him a nomination for an ASC (American Society of Cinematographers) Award. His first major studio film was 2007's *300*, directed by Zack Snyder, which commenced his professional relationship with Snyder. Fong would later work under Snyder on *Watchmen* (2009), *Suckerpunch* (2011) and *Batman Vs Superman* (2015). In 2011, the year he worked on *Super 8*, he was accepted into the American Society of Cinematographers.

Principal photography started in autumn 2010 and filming took place from September to October. The teaser trailer was filmed separately in April 2011. *Super 8* was partly shot in Weirton, West Virginia and during the four weeks they were there the locals were hospitable and kind. Weirton had been hit hard by a downturn, like so many small-town industrial parts of America. Abrams had to shoot a few unplanned scenes because of the weather, including a town hall meeting. Locals turned up at the last hour to be part of the scene. People who had never acted before were suddenly in a major Hollywood movie. Weirton was exactly what Abrams envisaged for his movie – the huge steel mill, the Main Street and the suburban neighbourhoods. He loved the idea of making a movie about kids and childhood innocence set against the backdrop of a huge factory. As the main character's mother was killed at the mill in a terrible accident, it was a constant reminder of the tragic event.

There are some incredible visual stunts in the film, notably when the monster is unleashed from the train after the crash. The actors loved that scene because it was so much fun to shoot; but Abrams brought in stunt doubles for some of the more dangerous parts. They did several takes of the train crash. It was a teenager's dream to see explosions on a film set and Spielberg was there to watch the kids who got to run and dodge the explosions coming from the train and the army tanks. It was a total adrenaline rush. They had to have safety meetings first of course, and rehearse their actions before they filmed.

'Well, they blew the building up,' Courtney told *Screen Rant*'s Roth Cornet. 'So we weren't allowed to be there. But there was this one part where there were explosions behind us and we could do that, because we were nowhere near anything that was really dangerous. But when the building exploded and there was wood flying everywhere we weren't allowed to do that – because when they actually blew the building up we were two hundred yards away and still the shock wave hit us – it was immense. The shock was huge. Like I don't know what they blew it up with, but it was big – and it was crazy.'

'As the process went along I realised I had the potential makings of my favourite sort of movie, which is the one that is the hardest genre to define,' Abrams said to *LA Times*'s Geoff Boucher. 'That's because you could say – and be right – that it's a science-fiction movie; or you could say – and be right – that it's a love story; or you could say – and be right – that it's a comedy; or you could say – and be right – that it's a special-effects spectacle.

That sort of cocktail is for me what I love about movies… that was the beginnings of *this* movie coming together.'

Abrams spoke to *Radio Times*'s Andrew Collins about the feelings of nostalgia the film evokes: 'Revisiting that period was truly surreal, because there would be moments when I was on the set and I would find a *TV Guide* and I'd flip through it, and remember reading that cover-to-cover when I was a kid, or looking at some of those models, or games, or posters, or Wacky Packages cards, and having this weird sort of sense-memory of being in my room at that age... and about what was in the drawers... so the whole spirit of the movie was a throwback.'

The name 'Super 8' derives from the Eastman Kodak film format of the late 1960s, which became a huge sensation amongst budding filmmakers. It inspired the likes of Spielberg and his protégés Joe Dante, Robert Zemeckis and J.J. Abrams. He felt a yearning for the old pre-mobile phone and pre-VHS era with no downloads and instant technology. It was more creative in many respects. Filmmakers had to really think about how to get their ideas onto the big screen in the pre-CGI days.

Though Abrams prefers working with film, he is still a fan of digital. He is obsessed by all means of filmmaking. Old school filmmaking allows room for imagination on behalf of the viewer, whereas digital gives the viewer literally everything in a crisp, clear way; yet paradoxically, such clarity can become unreal, an alienating experience. (When Bob Dylan told *Rolling Stone* magazine in 2009 that all music made in the previous twenty years had been 'atrocious', this wasn't just the lament of a deaf oldster: digital tracks didn't sound right to him, they didn't sound 'real'.) Without modern technology the visual effects in *Super 8* could not have been made, the resources available in the 1970s could not cut it. Abrams loves modern technology but has a feeling for old-school filmmaking.

A common theme running through Spielberg's films is the emotional impact on a child whose parents have divorced, which happened to Spielberg. Abrams's parents, on the other hand, stayed married but he had friends whose parents separated, so he was able to draw from their experiences. Joe has of course lost his mother in *Super 8*. Spielberg was very helpful in the development of the story and allowed Abrams to make the movie that he originally envisaged while offering ideas. Spielberg also helped Abrams in the editing suite by spending hours with him. The pair became partners and collaborators.

There is a sense of innocence and wonder about that film that is lacking in modern movies. Much of it is not just to do with the era in which the film is set but also the actors. Inevitably with a bunch of kids on set they had a lot of fun. 'The best prank would have to be off-set,' Joel Courtney said to *Screen Rant*'s Roth Cornet. 'It was April fool's day… [laughing] J.J. will probably not ever forgive us for this one. Riley [Griffiths, who plays Charles in the film] told J.J. that he had left his script in a mall and that he couldn't find it and when he went back to look for it…it was gone. It gave J.J. like a heart attack. He was so scared, and then after a little while of just like freaking J.J. out – Riley's like, "April fools!"'

The film was kept a closely guarded secret; more than any other release of the year. 'I'm not trying to be coy or manipulative or Machiavellian, I want to spark people's imaginations,' said Abrams to *GQ*'s Stuart McGurk. 'We live in an age of instant knowledge. And there's almost a sense of entitlement to that. Some resent it, they're so used to every damn piece of information the second they want it. So I feel like, you know, it's not a bad exercise to be told, no, this piece of information you can't have right now.'

'It wasn't too hard to keep the secret,' Ryan Lee said to *Screen Rant*'s Roth Cornet, 'because I love knowing secrets and I had promised J.J. and Bryan Burk personally that I would. So that's a really big responsibility. When I do know a secret, I keep it that way. And besides – if I had spilled the beans, I fear that my punishment would be far worse than going to bed without dinner forever.'

Fans had to glean what they could from the teaser trailer, which was basically a train derailment and some sort of monster escaping from a military train car. Abrams wanted the release of *Super 8* to be like a voyage of discovery, which is why he kept the film under wraps for so long.

Abrams told *Time Out* Japan's David Fear, 'For me, a lot of the fun of trailers used to be that often, you never knew something was being made until you saw these coming-attractions previews – and then you had all these speculations and hopes about what the actual movie would be like when you finally would get to see it. Now, it's: "Oh, yeah, I remember that from the behind-the-scenes pictures online, or I knew that moment was coming from the set report they showed on TV."'

'I enjoyed going to *Super 8*,' British actor and future Abrams collaborator Benedict Cumberbatch told an audience of journalists at a London press conference, 'and not knowing anything about it and I kind of, without patronising an audience, would say it's equivalent to giving a kid a whole box of chocolates as opposed to just a few. And they'll enjoy the few, hopefully; if they eat the whole box they'll throw up and forget about it.'

Abrams spoke to Geoff Boucher of *Hero Complex*, the pop culture section of the *LA Times*: 'To me, all people need to know is that it's an adventure about a small town and it's funny, it's sweet, it's scary and there's a mystery: What is this thing that has escaped? What are the ramifications of its presence? And what is the effect on people? But I know that's not enough. Look, I feel we need a little bit of a coming-out party because we are up against massive franchises and brands and most people don't know what *Super 8* means. We're a complete anomaly in a summer of huge films…and we don't want to be so silent or coy that people don't care or don't hear about it.'

Coming directly after making *Mission: Impossible III* Abrams could not help but feel the transition from a big movie with a hefty budget, the biggest star and a global franchise to a relatively modest movie with unnamed actors and a nostalgic story. But Abrams is a filmmaker who is interested in story and content first and foremost, rather than visuals.

Abrams explained to *Time Out* Japan's David Fear: 'The fundamental pressure is the same whether it's a name brand or something unknown. Which is: God, I really hope I didn't screw this up! [Laughs] But it becomes that much harder to get people into the theatre when, for most moviegoers, that title has no resonance – "*Super 8*? Is it some sort of a superhero movie?" Really, it's a complete cipher even if you're aware that it's referring to a film stock. We have great actors but no one that's a household name, and we're not doing anything based on a pre-existing character or novel. There's nothing here that you can rely on to generate interest simply by association.'

'I am still terrified by everything I do, what the reaction will be. The confidence [the *Super 8* filmmakers] have is something I would see in friends of mine from school, and just …where the hell does that come from!' Abrams confessed to Jessica Furseth of *Idol Magazine*.

During production Abrams's mother was diagnosed with cancer. 'It was a very weird thing to be working on something about a boy dealing with the loss of his mother while that was going on for real,' he confessed to *The Guardian*'s Andrew Pulver.

*Super 8* was released (as a Bad Robot and Amblin Entertainment production with distribution by Paramount) in June 2011 and received positive reviews from critics and grossed $260 million worldwide after a budget of $50 million.

Looking back on the film and how it might have changed his world, Ryan Lee told Roth Cornet of *Screen Rant*: 'J.J., Steven, the cast, and I were all having dinner and J.J. said to us, "Cherish these moments because soon you're not going to be able to go out without being noticed." But it's kind of hard for me to wrap my head around what might come. But whatever it is, I'm ready for the adventure.'

'Too much thick-throated emotion is stirred into the wondrous, mawkish finale,' commented Jamie Graham in his *Total Film* magazine review. 'The blend of sentiment and spectacle here evokes Spielberg at his worst as well as his best, and the film's subtext is heavily underlined in case we missed it. But even this bum note at the end of a too-frantic third act won't stop *Super 8* from being, hands down, the film of the summer. Only a young Spielberg at the top of his game could beat it.'

Chris Tookey wrote in the *Daily Mail*: 'This ingenious mixture of charming-rites-of-passage children's movie with science-fiction-monster-spectacular is better than the other summer blockbusters this year by the same kind of margin that the England cricket team humbled India at Trent Bridge. J.J. Abrams' *Super 8* is not just the most entertaining family film of the summer, it's up there with the classics of its various genres.'

'Still, "not as good as *E.T.*" is not so bad. ("Better than *Thor* or *X-Men: First Class*" may be a more relevant judgment at this moment in the history of air-conditioning),' wrote A.O. Scott in his review of the film in *The New York Times*. 'You know that, in the homestretch, big battles will be fought, lessons will be learned, the elusive monster will be revealed and other loose ends will be tied up. You may wish it did not all happen in such a perfunctory, predictable way. The machinery of genre, in other words, so ingeniously kept to a low background hum for so long, comes roaring to life, and the movie enacts its own loss of innocence. *Super 8* turns out, the way many of us turn out, not to be so special after all.'

The last word on the film should perhaps be from Abrams, as he lays out the challenges faced by the film in finding its audience: 'We have such a challenge on this movie,' Abrams told *LA Times*'s Geoff Boucher. 'Yes, we've got Steven's name on it and my name on it – for what that's worth – but we've got no famous super-hero, we've got no pre-existing franchise or sequel, it's not starring anyone you've heard of before. There's no book, there's no toy, there's no comic book. There's nothing.

I don't have anything; I don't even have a board game, that's how bad it is. But I think we have a very good movie.' And that was enough.

In 2011 Abrams produced *Mission: Impossible – Ghost Protocol*, another high-concept action thriller starring Tom Cruise as IMF Agent Ethan Hunt.

'I love the adventure of the character,' Cruise said to *IndieLondon*'s Jack Foley on the subject of the *Mission: Impossible* series and returning to his role as Ethan Hunt. 'I love the world that you can create and you can always go to a different place – different locations and there's always a new mission. It's tremendously challenging to put these films together. I love adventure movies, I just love action adventure films. It's pure cinema and you go in and you're lost to it. To me, it's that challenge – I want to give an audience that ride, that entertainment. That's what I love about *Mission: Impossible*, as soon as you hear that theme tune it gets you. And you know, it's the promise of summer. It's going to be a great summer and I want to contribute to that.'

First time feature director Brad Bird had moved from animated films such as *The Iron Giant*, *The Incredibles* and *Ratatouille*, so the media were focusing on whether he could handle such a big Hollywood live action production or not.

'He's a filmmaker who has happened to use animation as a medium,' Abrams told MTV, 'but it's his filmmaking and his characters and his rhythm and his comedy, the action he can do, it's just the humanity that he's done that comes through in movies that have happened to be animated. Seeing that kind of nuance in a movie with people is just, I'm just so thrilled to be a part of it all. I haven't seen the whole thing, but what I have seen is sort of mind-blowing.'

Cruise was impressed by Bird's storytelling and style as shown in *The Incredibles* and called Bird from Tokyo after its release to express his admiration for the film and to tell him that if he ever wanted to direct a live action film to give him a call. Bird went on to an aborted film called *1906* and then directed 2007's animated feature *Ratatouille*.

Some time after Cruise's phone call, Bird had lunch at the Bad Robot offices and Abrams walked by and asked him what he was up to. The two filmmakers had known each other for a long time but had never had the opportunity to work together. Bird told him he was looking around for another project. That night, Bird got a text message from Abrams (the pair had once shared the same agent) which read 'Mission?' Bird was intrigued.

'I think that one of the things Tom set out to do,' Bird told *Movieline*'s Julie Miller, 'which I think is very enlightened for the franchise, is to have each film take on the stamp of the director. I think the reason he decided to do that is because he likes working with directors with specific, pronounced points of view. That's part of what attracted me to this. I thought that was cool because then I'm not trying to fit into someone else's [directing] style. I'm doing what I think would be a cool *Mission: Impossible*. One of the earliest things J.J. asked me was, "What things would you love to see in a spy movie?" I pitched several things and several of those things ended up in the movie.'

Bird elaborated on the point to Drew Taylor of *Indiewire*: 'The other thing that attracted me to this was Tom's desire, from the first *Mission: Impossible* film on, to have each film in the series have the style of its director. So the ones that Brian De Palma, and J.J. and John Woo did were all distinctly different from each other, even though they're all *Mission: Impossible* films, which meant that I had some elbow room to make my own kind of film, which was attractive to me.'

Adam Goodman, the president of Paramount, was with Cruise and Abrams in wanting Bird to direct the fourth *Mission: Impossible* film. However, some of the chiefs at Paramount were a little worried that Bird may have been out of his depth, but as soon as they saw some early footage their misgivings evaporated and they became fully committed to Bird as director. In fact, on location across the globe Bird's background in animation helped him because with animation you have to visualise meticulously before filming.

'…I've been wanting to do live action for a long time, absolutely,' he confessed to *The A.V. Club*'s Tasha Robinson. 'But it was daunting, because it was a really physically large production. It was larger than the last *Mission: Impossible*, but it had a smaller budget and a tighter schedule, so it was both bigger and sort of lean at the same time. That was a challenge.'

It was written by André Nemec and Josh Appelbaum and working with Abrams and Cruise they created lots of interesting set pieces and sequences. The initial working title of the feature was (totally out of left field) *Mission: Impossible 4* with the codename 'Aries' during the earlier stages of production. One idea was for the franchise name *Mission: Impossible* to be axed from the title, like Christopher Nolan's *Batman* sequel *The Dark Knight*. Principal photography started in October 2010 and filming finished in March the following year. It took the cast and crew to Mumbai, Prague, Moscow, Vancouver, Bangalore and Dubai.

'I like to work with people that I like hanging out with,' Cruise told *Examiner*'s Carla Hay of working with J.J. Abrams on the fourth film, 'that I admire, that are really smart and talented, and we can problem solve together. That's what it's about. I love J.J. So to work with him on this [movie], that's why I did it. I brought it to him and said, "Let's do this together. We'll have some fun."'

*Mission: Impossible* had by now become one of the most lucrative film franchises in history. It was as if each film was destined to become a box office smash. Cruise's megastar power had waned in recent years but audiences had invested in the character of Ethan Hunt and the big screen *Mission: Impossible* films. There's no question that the films launched the live action feature length directing careers of both J.J. Abrams and Brad Bird. Both filmmakers value story and character development over action scenes and special effects. Ultimately, it is the story which will stand the test of time, whereas visual effects of any sort can easily date as new technology is invented.

'It's so weird,' Abrams said to MTV about Bird, 'to watch scenes for a movie by a director that feels so of that director's style, and yet you realise you've never ever seen a live-action film by that director. You watch moments where you go, "That's so Brad Bird!" And then you realise, "Oh, it's so weird to have seen a Brad Bird moment with actual flesh-and-blood actors."'

Cruise told *Examiner*'s Carla Hay of his admiration for Bird: 'His sequences are amazing. And also his characters, how he keeps the tension and suspense in his stories. When you look at *The Incredibles*, when you look at *Ratatouille*, the design of those sequences, the characters and also his understanding and love of cinema. We share that together. When we got together, we just talked about...You just go right in. It's like an old friend talking about our favourite movies and things. And I felt personally that he was someone I'd really like to hang out with and work with, and someone I have great respect for.'

Cinematographer Robert Elswit and editor Paul Hirsch helped Bird deliver arguably the best *Mission: Impossible* film in the series. In terms of set pieces it was the biggest movie of the franchise, yet the script was evolving while they were making it. The schedule was as tight as a piano wire. The days were long and they didn't even have prep time. The head of the stunt team, Gregg Smrz, had his work cut out, as the film needed even more action scenes and stunts than the average Hollywood action movie. Abrams and Cruise were very supportive and let Bird do whatever he wanted with the film.

Bird told *The A.V. Club*'s Tasha Robinson: 'I can't name another actor who's worked with that many different kinds of directors, and he's learned from every single one of them. His film knowledge is vast, and that goes from technical issues to creative issues.'

There is a playfulness that is different from the other *Mission: Impossible* films and certainly a deeper focus on characters than in the first two movies in the series. It seems to be funnier than the previous three films. The humour, though, does not detract from the action scenes or suspense. Both Abrams's film and Bird's are reminiscent of *Raiders of the Lost Ark*, the first *Indiana Jones* film, in that they evenly balance the right amount of humour and action.

It was released in December, a little more than a year after filming started and was an instant critical and commercial success. It became the highest-grossing Tom Cruise film thus far, with a worldwide gross of close to $700 million.

Tim Robey wrote a positive review in *The Daily Telegraph*: 'Still, a lot of credit goes to Cruise here, who's succeeded over these four films in making Ethan Hunt into a strangely intriguing alter ego. Hunt, like Cruise, is itchily uncomfortable in his own skin – they're both drawn to disguise – and we spot signs of fatigue, of here-we-go-again, which give him mature grit and appeal.'

'Loosely wired together by *Alias* scribes Josh Appelbaum and André Nemec, *Ghost* is really just a chain reaction of incredible set-pieces,' wrote Jonathan Crocker in *Total Film*. 'In fact, the film never recovers from the adrenaline-comedown of its extraordinary Dubai sequence. Stacking scenes on top of each other, Bird keeps the movie flexing relentlessly between hold-your-breath tension and open-throttle action. Double-deception, shootout, brawl, Cruise hurtling through a chaotic sandstorm... it's the best Bond film never made.'

Philip French wrote in *The Observer*: 'The plot is much the same as that in the latest *Sherlock Holmes* picture, though the aim here is the quite literal end of civilisation as we know it so that a newly cleansed world can open up for mankind. This is the best movie in the franchise since Brian De Palma launched it in 1996, and the director is Brad Bird, an animator by training, who made Pixar's *Ratatouille* and *The Incredibles*.'

What about Abrams's opinion of the film?

'I think it's the best one of the series,' he exclaimed to *Collider*'s Christina Radish. 'I do. First of all, you've never seen a live action Brad Bird movie, and yet when you watch it, you go, "This is a Brad Bird movie." You realise you've been watching Brad Bird films that just happen to be animated. It's really fun. It's got a fun intensity to it, and that's Brad. It's the biggest one, by far, in terms of the stuff that happens in it. Also, there are other things like a portion of it was shot in IMAX and there's a sequence on the tallest building in the world, the Burj in Dubai, where Tom Cruise did five days' worth of wire work outside the building that is so insane, you cannot believe the insurance company let him do it. When you see it on IMAX, it's terrifying. It's crazy, what he did. It really is unbelievable. It's weird to be in meetings with him and think, "That dude was running down the outside of the building!" I'm talking to him, he's in my office, and he did that. It's weird. It's like talking to Buzz Aldrin. You're like, "That dude was on the moon!"'

Cruise (star and producer on the movie) and the studio were hit by a lawsuit when screenwriter Timothy Patrick McLanahan claimed that Cruise and Paramount studio used his as yet un-filmed 1998 screenplay *Head On* as the basis for *Ghost Protocol.* The film grossed an eventual $1b in worldwide sales including box-office tickets, DVDs, Blu-rays, subscription costs and merchandise. It became the highest grossing film in the franchise. McLanahan claimed the lot. The suit was filed at the US district court in Los Angeles in February 2014. The suit claimed that McLanahan delivered his screenplay to the famed Hollywood agency William Morris in 1998 but it was rejected. McLanahan argued that William Morris passed the script onto Cruise via his agent Rick Nicita at CAA and his producer partner Paula Wagner without his permission or knowledge. When McLanahan saw the film several years later he 'immediately recognised that the scripts for this movie had been illegally written and produced from *Head On*'s 1998 copyright.'

Bert Fields, Cruise's lawyer, dismissed the lawsuit when he spoke to *AFP*. 'Tom Cruise has never stolen anything from anyone. This bizarre lawsuit against thirteen people will be quickly dismissed by the court.' Well, fairly quickly: the lawsuit was dropped that July.

Abrams continued to make his mark on genre TV and served as executive producer of the cult series *Person of Interest* in 2011. Abrams has a good relationship with Fox, which is just as well with so many TV projects on the go. Not all of them can work. He simply pursues those things that interest him.

'It's a very funny thing, I had lunch a few years ago with Paul Simon, Simon and Garfunkel,' he told PBS's Tavis Smiley, 'and I was talking about this very thing...He was amazing. He was saying how that for a while, the stuff that interested him did interest people. They were top of the charts, they were revolutionary in a lot of ways as musicians. He said, "Then sometimes you get to a place and not everyone reacts." I think it's not about when your time is and isn't, and people have ups and downs. I think you can't predict anything. You don't know what anyone's going to say.'

Abrams left the day-to-day running of the show in the capable hands of its creator and Greg Plageman. If there were any issues about character and story Abrams would offer a helping hand but other than that he stayed out of the way and let them get on with it. He saw the dailies and read the scripts and gave notes but watched the series like any other viewer.

Abrams learned that once you find talented and creative people the best thing to do is let them carry on with it.

The show was created by Jonathan Nolan, brother of *The Dark Night* and *Inception* director Christopher Nolan. 'Jonah [Jonathan Nolan's nickname] pitched an amazing story and I just found myself like a kid at a campfire, wanting to hear more,' Abrams explained to Abbie Bernstein of *Buzzy Mag*. 'We were actually talking about a movie at the time. And then he pitched this idea for a TV show and I screamed and grabbed the people who are repping me on TV to hear this idea. And then he wrote a great script.'

Aaron Riccio wrote of the first season in *Slant Magazine*: 'There isn't a single interesting person in CBS's dud-on-arrival *Person of Interest*; at best, there's only a single interesting idea.'

'Despite the presence of Nolan (who's co-written most of his brother Christopher's films, including *Memento* and *The Prestige*) and producer J.J. Abrams,' said Dan Fienberg in *Hitfix*, 'this is very much a CBS crime procedural, one that could fit comfortably alongside *The Mentalist*, et al. But it would help an awful lot if Caviezel had a few Red Bulls first.'

Nevertheless, it's still going strong at the time of writing in its fourth season in 2015 and renewed for a fifth. *Person of Interest* is a science-fiction crime drama starring Jim Caviezel as a former CIA agent recruited by an elusive billionaire (played by Michael Emerson of *Lost* fame) to prevent crimes from happening in New York City. Abrams was intrigued by the idea of surveillance and had always of course been fascinated by spies. Nolan wanted to explore the concept of surveillance in a world of ubiquitous CCTV, online snooping and social media. People have become so accustomed to cameras in the street that they have forgotten they exist. The question is: who is behind those cameras?

All this was happening in the background as Abrams was beaming back up into space.

CHAPTER 9

# BACK TO THE *ENTERPRISE*

'You have to literally change the way you consider orienting the audience.'

**J.J. Abrams, *The Quietus*, 2009**

Abrams went back to *Star Trek* with the release of *Star Trek Into Darkness* in 2013. After the fourth *Mission: Impossible* film and various bits of TV work, Abrams had begun focusing on the story and character development for his second *Star Trek* film; sorting out the cast and crew before they began talking about locations, wardrobe and visual effects, the budget and so forth.

'There have been a lot of things that we've been working on,' Abrams explained to *Collider*'s Christina Radish prior to the making of the film, 'a lot of important elements that we just know we need to really nail down and solve. Once you say, "We're ready to go, but we don't have a finished script yet," or "I'm directing the thing and here's the release date, but we don't have a finished script," what starts to happen – and I've seen this happen with a lot of friends of mine – is that you're suddenly in production on a movie that they're thinking, "Oh my god, we weren't really ready. We thought we'd get it done in time, but we didn't." So, while we have a moment to say, "Let's get the important things figured out," then all the pre-production stuff will come.'

Directed by Abrams and written by Roberto Orci, Alex Kurtzman and Damon Lindelof – whose film credits now included not only *Star Trek* but *Cowboys & Aliens* and *Prometheus* plus the Marvel comic book mini-series *Ultimate Wolverine vs. Hulk* – it is the thirteenth film in the *Star Trek* franchise. By this point Kurtzman and Orci had racked up a significant CV and had become known as 'Hollywood's Secret Weapons'. The previous six years' worth of films, including *The Island*, *The Legend Of Zorro*, *Mission: Impossible III*, *Transformers* and its sequel *Transformers: Revenge of the Fallen*, and also *Cowboys & Aliens*, had grossed over $3 billion at the box office. Kurtzman had made his directorial debut with 2012's *People Like Us*.

*Star Trek* is not only about spectacle but story and characters and lifelong *Star Trek* fans Orci and Kurtzman knew this all too well, which is why they were so protective over the script for the 2009 film and why they'd take the same approach to the sequel, with Lindelof on board as co-writer.

'We didn't want to do a sequel just to do a sequel, which happens a lot in our industry, where unfortunately, it just feels like the conveyer belt keeps moving. So we wanted to make sure we wanted to do the movie, and not to do it for the sake of doing it,' Burk told *BringMeTheNews*'s Tim Lammers. 'There were a lot of conversations about, "How do we raise the bar for people who came to watch the last one?" We really wanted to get it right.'

Paramount Pictures had been interested in making a second

new *Star Trek* film back in June 2008 and by March 2009 they had the creators of the first Abrams film on board. 'They set a date,' Kurtzman told *Collider*'s Steve 'Frosty' Weintraub, 'and we all felt strongly that we did not want to make the movie if we didn't feel that we could match the enthusiasm and love that we brought to the first one. To put the movie out to just meet a date would not have been the way to make the movie. I think we owe too much to the fans and to ourselves to not do it that way. We really wanted to take our time until we felt that we had a story that we could stand behind and that we felt was worthy of a sequel.'

Of course, fans were left wondering if due to the success of *Star Trek* there would be a new TV series but the chiefs at Paramount and CBS were obviously all too aware that saturating the market with too much *Star Trek* material would ruin the potential box-office success of another big-screen movie. Certainly two successful movies would indicate a return in fortunes of the franchise, so perhaps a TV series is a possibility in the long-term.

Abrams was asked about his thoughts on being involved with a new *Star Trek* TV series. 'I don't know,' Abrams said to Abbie Bernstein of *Buzzy Mag* at the time. 'It's never really come up. Depending on what that would be, and how it would be done, I'd be open to the idea of it, but right now, we're just sort of focusing on making a movie that's worth people's time.'

An initial script was finished by Christmas 2009 for a possible 2011 release. 'There's a lot of baton-handing off since it's just difficult for any of us to be in one place at one time, so at any given time, there's two or three of us making *Trek* their full-time job, and the others are going off and focusing their attention on another of our projects,' Lindelof admitted to *BringMeTheNews* journalist Tim Lammers. 'That process is very exciting and very reminiscent of the way it works in television. That collaboration is what made the first movie work and we wanted to make sure we recaptured the same lightning in a bottle this time around.'

'We are such a part of a team on *Trek* in terms of how it's a development that we share with J.J., Damon, and Bryan Burk,' Orci said to *Collider*'s Steve 'Frosty' Weintraub. 'So, yeah, you do have to keep notes and remember your stuff because it's a band and when you get together to practice you want everyone to have done their homework a little bit as opposed to when it is just me and Alex in an office every day usually.'

Press reports circulated as to the film's concept, though Leonard Nimoy had stated that he would not be returning to reprise his role as Spock Prime. Some reports suggested that Abrams was considering bringing in the original Kirk, William Shatner. Another idea that the writers floated around was to have the film split into two parts, as Christopher Nolan did with his *Dark Knight* sequels. Abrams and cohorts found it difficult creating a villain for the film, though the favourite possibility was to bring back Khan Noonien Singh and the Klingons from *Star Trek II: The Wrath of Khan*, undoubtedly the best film of the original six *Star Trek* movies.

Eric Bana was fantastic as the first film's villain but they wanted to expand the role of the bad guy in the second film, believing that sequels are all about the villains. Khan is such a good villain in the *Star Trek* universe because, like the best villains, the audience learns his back story and can become emotionally engaged in the story and even empathise. After losing his wife he goes crazy and the audience begins to understand why he is so deranged. Khan is a character without a conscience: pure evil. It is not quite so clear cut with the Romulan Nero, who is a villain from the future, whereas Khan is from the *Trek*'s past, so he is familiar to the audience.

'The old adage that your hero is only as good as your villain is true,' Orci told *Den of Geek*'s Simon Brew. 'But uniquely with sequels, the first film in a franchise is about setting up the world, but in this one, it's who puts the crew to the test? Who forces Kirk to become the captain that he is? Did he inherit the chair too early? If so, what's going to happen when he's faced with a real challenge, and an enemy that he doesn't know what to do with?'

The writers brought in an ensemble cast of peripheral yet important characters such as Christopher Pike, the original Enterprise captain, Carol Marcus, and Spock's father Sarek. They were also detailed enough in their research to avoid any potential howlers with the timeline as evidenced in *Star Trek II: The Wrath of Khan*, which sees Chekov reacquaint himself with Khan, when in fact the pair had never met in the original series first season episode 'Space Seed' because Chekov was not introduced until season two.

They had made it clear with the 2009 film that they were not going to be using Khan but the question of who exactly the villain was going to be would crop up again for the sequel and even casual fans were bombarding Abrams and the writers with questions about Khan and his possible inclusion in the sequel. Abrams and the writers got together in the Bad Robot offices and discussed the pros and cons of using Khan. The downside of having him was that he'd been used before and to great effect in the second big screen *Star Trek* movie, so the writers of *Into Darkness* had to be sure they'd do him justice.

After the release of *Super 8* Abrams, Lindelof, Orci and Kurtzman got together to devise a story that included Khan against the backdrop of what happened after the planet Vulcan blew up in the first film. Familiarity would be key to the success of the film but there would also be a challenge in bringing something new to the script that would be accepted by fans.

Though the idea of using Khan as the villain for the sequel may have seemed predictable, the writers wanted the story built around some far-reaching concepts – including the meaning of friendship and the threat of terrorism. They needed a bad guy to match the bold ideas. Khan made Spock understand what Kirk meant when he talked about friendship. Kirk breaks Federation rules for the good of his crew. In many ways the writers were testing Roddenberry's idea of a utopian future that can only exist if all alien species work together to explore space. The writers felt that Khan would put Kirk to the ultimate test, push his buttons and provoke his instincts. Kirk believes in friendship and putting the lives of his ship and crew first and he does not believe in a no-win scenario. Khan has similar ideas about ship and crew, so he proved to be the perfect foe for the sequel – but they knew they had to do something different from *The Wrath of Khan* because it is such a revered film.

'One of the guiding forces in the first movie that we always asked each other was "as fans of this, what would we want to see?"' Lindelof explained to *TrekMovie.com*'s Anthony Pascale. '…We want new stuff that we have never seen before, but we also want the familiar items on the menu because those are the things we love to eat. And if there is a way we can bring both of those together in harmony so it doesn't feel like they don't fit, then that becomes a sort of mission statement. So there have to be moments in anything we do in *Trek* where 10 per cent of the audience chuckles at a reference or a visual cue or a planetary system that we are paying homage to, but the other 90 per cent of the audience can go along for the ride too. It is just finding that balance so it's not too inside, but it's inside enough so that the people that have invested the last forty years of their lives in this incredible myth feel like they are getting their money's worth.'

The destruction of Vulcan changed Starfleet, an organization that represents peace and whose sole aim is to explore and expand mankind's knowledge by discovering new worlds but, as the Prime Directive states, they cannot intervene in the evolution of alien cultures; they must simply gain knowledge and wisdom as outsiders. With *Star Trek Into Darkness* the writers posed questions such as: what would happen if earth was attacked? What would happen if Starfleet was compromised? *Star Trek Into Darkness* became as much about rescuing Starfleet as anything else. 'In order for it to make sense, our crew had to be tempted by the spirit of vengeance,' Lindelof said to *BringMeTheNews*'s Tim Lammers. 'Would they have the moral dilemma if someone killed somebody or provoked an action against somebody who had done something horrible to innocents? We had to explore that and what it would take to bring them back to that original vision of hopefulness, peace and camaraderie. But obviously in order to get there, you have to move to this very, very dark place.'

They wanted Khan to be a surprise; John Harrison and the

writers must have had Darth Vader in mind and the revelation in *The Empire Strikes Back* that he is Luke Skywalker's father.

'If everything you know going into the movie is "It's a guy named Khan,"' Burk told *Slash Film*'s Germain Lussier, 'even if you don't even know who Khan is, you know that you're watching a film where for forty-five minutes or an hour of the movie you are ahead of the characters, so you're just kind of waiting for them to catch up with what you already know, that he is not who he says he is. So there's the general idea of going to see a movie and allowing it to unfold as it normally does.'

'Because there was so much scrutiny on what we were going to do,' Kurtzman admitted to *I Am Rogue*'s Jami Philbrick, 'we felt like it's our responsibility to ask people to come to the theatre and hopefully know very little and we'll get to surprise them. They'll get to be wide-eyed and wondered again when they come to the movies. Some people just reject that and say, "That is not the world we live in anymore. I need to know everything before I go in or I'm going to hate it." That's okay, if that's the way you want it, everybody has a right. But it's our feeling that you go to the movies for wonderment and discovery, and we didn't want to rob anybody of that. We didn't want to be "cool and secretive," we more just wanted to protect a dying art form now.'

In December 2010 Abrams said he wasn't sure if he was going to direct the next *Star Trek* film because there was still no script. In February 2011 Orci tweeted that he planned to deliver the script in March. Paramount had already begun bankrolling pre-production without a script.

The writers, Kurtzman and Orci, were initially sceptical

about delving into the *Star Trek* universe, being major fans of the franchise and not wanting to potentially ruin it or upset the fans. They had talked about working on a *Trek* movie in the past but nothing serious came of it until they started talking to Paramount.

'Frankly we had an idea and we thought "man, this actually might work,"' Orci told *Geek Monthly* magazine's Anthony Pascale. 'We actually locked into it once we had an idea of what we wanted to do. Once you have an idea, it is hard to ignore it. It stays in your mind and you think "wow if we don't do it, then someone might come in and ruin it." It was both defensive and inspired by an idea of what we thought *Star Trek* needed.'

They knew they wanted to go back to the original characters and their back stories, though they faced lots of chronology problems as they knew the outcome of the original characters (such as Kirk's death in the seventh film, *Generations*) so they had to think of ways of how to handle that.

Fans wondered what was going to happen with the new film because by April, Orci had said at WonderCon that the film's final first draft had been submitted. Abrams stated that after he completed *Super 8* he would turn his full time and attention to *Star Trek*. The film's schedule was pushed back for a June 2012 release and by September 2011 Abrams finally confirmed he was to direct *Star Trek Into Darkness*. The title indicated where the story was headed. It would be a stand-alone film and not a two-parter as initially discussed and reported.

'It was the cast originally, because I just wanted to work with them again,' Abrams told *Geek Nation*'s Ben Pearson when asked what enticed him to return to direct a second *Star Trek* film. 'But then we started talking about what the story would be, I was just getting very excited about the possibilities of doing – the idea of being able to bring Khan back. The idea of this black stealth version of the Enterprise was interesting to me. The idea of doing a chase scene in San Francisco. The idea of having a future San Francisco. It was a bunch of elements.'

The cast of the first Abrams-directed Star Trek feature reprised their roles as the crew of the USS *Enterprise*. The story takes place twelve months after the first film, where Kirk and his crew are sent to the Klingon home world to locate former Starfleet officer-turned-terrorist John Harrison, played by *Sherlock* actor Benedict Cumberbatch. They were looking for an actor who could play a villain who didn't feel two-dimensional.

'I think it's obvious that your heroes are only as good as your villains,' Burk told the *San Diego Reader*'s Matthew Lickona. 'As we started talking about this character, he became even more insidious because he was coming from inside. Then, when we cast Benedict Cumberbatch, he became not only a formidable enemy to Kirk, but significantly smarter and more ruthless. He became the kind of villain that we love in the movies we see.'

Lindelof had seen *Sherlock* and recommended Cumberbatch to Abrams, who had not yet seen the acclaimed BBC production. He checked out *Sherlock* and was impressed. They sent some pages to Cumberbatch who auditioned and he was offered the part. Oddly enough, Cumberbatch auditioned for the role on an iPhone because the original camera he had didn't work. 'I had to do it with my best friend Adam, in his kitchen, with his wife videoing it on top of two chairs, crouched down, a table lamp for a little bit of "direct light", as we call it in the trade,' he explained to an audience of journalists at a London Q&A. 'And I literally was like that for the whole of the three scenes, I think we did. Two versions of each and, I dunno, we were doing it at about 10.30 p.m. and we stopped at midnight.'

They recorded it on a large file, took a day or so to compress it and sent it to Abrams, who was on holiday at the time. Abrams got back in touch with Cumberbatch to say he was happy with the audition. Cumberbatch received the news in January 2012 and was ecstatic over his first major film role.

'I didn't have qualms about any nationality but I had qualms about not having the best possible actor,' Abrams said to *It's Art Mag*. 'He is someone who just elevated everything and while you don't want the classic, clichéd British villain, which we've all seen a million times, my guess is that we've seen just as many American villains. I think Benedict is one of the best actors alive. So the real question is "why did he accept the movie?" I think he is so good and seeing him in *Sherlock* just blew my mind and I had that feeling that he would be great for almost anything. And he exceeded all my expectations.'

With Cumberbatch the writers wanted to create a classic villain; someone unforgettable who would stay in the audience's minds. Cumberbatch played Khan as the typical Shakespearian bad guy who's cunning, manipulative, intimidating, dominant and scary, aloof, someone who you can't keep your eyes off. 'I think the thing was that Khan really is the most iconic villain of the series,' Abrams said to

*Spinoff Online*'s Todd Gilchrist, 'and it felt like an opportunity to see another side of Khan and…like the first film did, use elements that people were familiar with but in a new way. It's a valid argument that it's about time for them to go off and discover and see things that have nothing to do with what we've seen before, and I think we'll always have some overlap. But I'm excited about the next chapter.'

Abrams saw Kirk and Khan as similar characters in some respects – two people who loved their crew and were dedicated to their jobs. They were passionate and tenacious. Khan was more of a complex villain than the angry Romulan from the first film. The writers kept Khan out of the pre-publicity press; neither confirming nor denying that Cumberbatch was Khan. '…I think at the end of the day, the withholding of story elements for me is something I would far rather have as an audience member than someone ruining a good first or second-act twist,' he explained to *Spinoff Online*'s Todd Gilchrist. 'But look, for people who want to have that information in advance, there's no shortage of access to that information if you want to see it. And I'm sure anybody who wanted to know before they went to the theatre knew that it was Khan.'

Paramount had never spent as much on a *Star Trek* film as they had with the two Abrams movies. With the 2009 film neither the producers nor the studio knew how the audience were going to react to a new *Star Trek* film or how the *Star Trek* purists were going to greet it.

'Then there were a group of people who, in the past, have rejected *Star Trek*,' Kurtzman said to *Den of Geek*'s Simon Brew, 'because it was too cold, too sci-fi, too unemotional, all of the things that we knew to be false about *Star Trek.* So we said alright, we need to bring those people in too. Because we are making a movie for a much bigger group. That, I think, ultimately has to do with telling stories that are about big universal emotions. *Trek* at its core, and Roddenberry in his vision for it, was always about reflecting the world we lived in, and the time that we lived in. But doing it in a way that was also emotional. That was the key for us: figuring out that balance. It is for the audience to decide if we found it, but that was certainly our collective goal.'

With *Into Darkness* they felt that if it was going to be the last *Star Trek* film they'd go out with a bang. They didn't have the financial resources to make it look as big as they wanted to so they used all sorts of filmic ideas and camera trickery to make it look much bigger than the 2009 film.

As with the first *Star Trek* film from 2009 there are lots of primary colours but the tone and look of the sequel shifts considerably to represent the dark forces in motion. The film explores some serious and critical issues that face Starfleet – and the whole of mankind. Interestingly, the title lacks a colon or a hyphen and so becomes a single phrase, mimicking the world plunging right into darkness. Yet the film still retains the optimism and vibe of the *Star Trek* universe.

'…my favourite *Trek* was *Next Generation*,' Lindelof told *Slash Film*'s Germain Lussier, 'and one of the things I loved about that show was that there was just a hardcore mystery element to the show and it usually took a good fifteen to twenty minutes for the *Enterprise* to figure out what the hell was going on. There would be strange things afoot that they had to figure out and obviously the original series also flirted with that in some of their best episodes. I think infusing that feeling of Kirk on the bridge with McCoy and Spock saying "What the hell is going on here?" is just something that really drives us and you know that we are big mystery fans in general, sometimes to our deficit, but we just can't avoid it and so that idea of keeping secrets is endemic to telling mystery stories.'

Viewers needed no prior knowledge of *Star Trek* to enjoy the film. It was made for those who had not seen anything set in the world of Starfleet and the USS *Enterprise*. It does not rely on any of the previous films and can be judged on its own merits. Nevertheless, it was still important to Abrams and the writers to honour what had come before it. As director, Abrams respected the fan base and wanted to make them happy. He knew it was important to embrace the original series but at the same time put his own spin on it. It was interesting for him to try to figure out how much to use from the original series and how much to disregard. It became a sort of balancing act. With both *Star Trek* films Abrams did not want to deny or reject elements of the show the fans love.

The writers wanted the sequel to connect the characters and the story to larger themes just as the original TV show had done in the 1960s. For the writers it wasn't a solid nine month-plus process for writing the script because though they had started work on the script in October 2010, by the summer of 2011 Kurtzman had directed *Welcome to People*, Lindelof was working on *Prometheus* and sometimes Burk was managing Bad Robot productions. *Star Trek* had not been their full-time job. They also produced some TV shows, too.

Rumours circulated on the net and amongst hardcore *Star Trek* fans that Abrams would start shooting the movie in

September 2012. He'd started shooting *Super 8* in September 2010 and it had to be released in June 2011 so he was used to tight schedules, but *Star Trek Into Darkness* needed a bigger post-production schedule than *Super 8* so Abrams was going to have to take more time. All parties concerned made a commitment to put out the best possible movie and not to rush anything for the sake of a schedule. The first film's original release date was Christmas but they pushed it back to the summer of 2009 so they could release the best movie that they could make. They were conscious that they wouldn't rush the film for the sake of it. It had to be a sequel that lived up to expectations – as sequels so rarely do.

Abrams began filming in January 2012 with visual effects completed by Industrial Light & Magic, the famed special effects company founded by *Star Wars* creator George Lucas. The film begins in London, though they didn't film there. The writers knew they wanted to use London as the opening city and though Starfleet Academy is based in San Francisco they did not want all the home planet scenes to be set there.

'I am such a *Star Trek* fan,' Orci admitted to *TrekMovie.com*'s Anthony Pascale about his reaction to the dailies (industry term for daily footage), 'that I'm not sure I would dislike anything we have shot so I'm not sure I'm a good source. I see them all in uniform on the ship and I'm like "Wow! This is great! New *Star Trek*!" But I'm the wrong guy to ask. But every few weeks during dailies I would see a new email chain go around with stuff like "Did you see that scene yesterday?" "Did you see Spock in that new close?" "Did you see Cumberbatch make it sound like poetry?" So to hear other people chattering about it is encouraging. And it's big. It's so big. It's epic. We just really went for a bigger version than we did last time, because of the trust.'

To the frustration of some fans the film was transferred to 3D during post production. Though Paramount wanted him to film in 3D, Abrams said he preferred to film in 2D but convert to 3D during production. Working in 3D was a new experience for him. Just as he was not a *Star Trek* fan before he worked on the 2009 film, the experience forced him to work in a new way.

'It's definitely the biggest film that any of us have worked with, that J.J. and I have worked on,' Bryan Burk told a crowd of journalists at a London Q&A, '... They're all new toys, particularly for J.J. and he didn't want to do it unless we could find new ways to play with them and try new things. So we're driving our 3D converter crazy – he's saying "You can't go any further!" and we keep saying "Come on, let's go further!" and he goes "But no one goes further than this!" and we're like "Come on, let's just push it a little further…" So we're breaking a lot of rules. And having fun doing it.'

Abrams approached 3D with misgivings because he gets a headache watching films in 3D and doesn't enjoy the experience of wearing 3D glasses. And 3D had become so incredibly popular that it felt almost like a fad. They shot *Star Trek Into Darkness* with anamorphic lenses so that it looked and felt like the 2009 film. (An anamorphic lens gives greater picture quality but distorts the image, stretching it vertically. The distortion is reversed by a complementary lens when the film is projected.)

'Yeah, I'm not like a 3D fanatic,' he said to *The Guardian*'s Horatia Harrod. 'I did feel pressure to do it on *Star Trek Into*

*Darkness*, but ultimately I understood why it was important to the studio. I was actually really glad in the long run that we did it that way, and I think it worked all right.'

Abrams is a fan of IMAX and chose to shoot thirty minutes in IMAX format.

'And within a month before shooting,' Burk said to journalists in London, 'maybe six weeks at the most, once everything was feeling like it was all going to start to work, we started talking about IMAX and we brought it up again and Brad Bird had such a wonderful experience shooting *Mission Impossible 4* on IMAX that we reopened the discussion and it was something that we started doing tests on. Basically, J.J. fell in love with it and it was one of those things where we managed to get everything inside the box and we popped back out because of IMAX.'

The scope of *Star Trek Into Darkness* is huge; far bigger in fact than the first film. Abrams wanted more scope and scale yet still to retain intimacy and emotion.

'3D is just an interesting format, you realise the limitations of shooting with 3D cameras,' Burk explained to *Digital Spy*'s Simon Reynolds, 'you realise the laborious process it takes to finish the film. Particularly if you don't want to just slap on 3D in post and really make it an experience. It takes a tremendous amount of manpower and great artists.' Still, they tried to build as many sets as they could because Abrams detests the idea of his actors standing in front of a blue screen, which is used with CGI technology. Production designer Scott Chambers, with whom Abrams has worked frequently since *Felicity*, made some incredible sets. It was important to Abrams to have the film look as authentic as possible, which is why so much of the production was shot on actual locations. The film has a feeling and look of reality.

'Everything has something it borrows from and certainly with the opening of this movie we were aware of a kind of nod to the opening of *Raiders of the Lost Ark*,' he told *It's Art Mag*. 'But really the spirit of the movie is that it's about a group of characters that I hope you like, that make you laugh and that you cheer for. If you are going to a place as intense as some of this stuff is in our movie, I think you need balance. There are moments that are pretty dark and crazy but those sequences won't matter to you, and you won't care about them, if you haven't been laughing along the way and rooting for these characters who you feel for.'

Abrams made the second film so that viewers did not have to see the 2009 movie, but it certainly adds to the experience knowing how the crew of the *Enterprise* came together. 'A lot of sequels, I think, fall into the trap of assuming that you care about the characters and assume you love them and are connected to them,' he said to *It's Art Mag*. 'Sometimes I see a sequel and the movie is starting and it assumes that I've just watched the other movie. So we tried to come at this from a stand-alone point of view. You don't have to have seen the other film but if you did, great and you'll understand how they all came together, but you don't need to. These characters have grown to love each other and that means the stakes are immediately higher and in *Star Trek Into Darkness* they are up against a formidable adversary.'

The first *Star Trek* film was an easier one to make in some ways because it was about introducing these characters to each other and to the audience, whereas with the second film the story had to take the characters to a new place. During the script development the writers had to make it so that each character had his or her own defining moment, an introduction as it were.

Abrams spoke to Scott Myers of *Playboy* about the differences between both *Trek* films. 'I learned so much doing the first *Star Trek*,' he said. 'I'd never done any kind of space adventure before or anything on that scale. We knew the second one had to be bigger and not just for bigger's sake. It was where the story was taking us. We got really cool glimpses of the *Enterprise* in the first movie. This time we get to see areas of the ship nobody's seen before. And the villain is more complex now. In our first film Eric Bana plays a wonderfully angry Romulan dude, pissed off and full of vengeance. In this one, the bad guy is still brutal and fierce, but he's got a much more interesting and active story. We have to grapple with many layers of his character. He's essentially a space terrorist, and Benedict Cumberbatch, who people know from BBC's *Sherlock*, is fucking kickass in the role. Kirk and the rest of the crew are figuring out how the hell to get an upper hand with this guy. The darkness is real in this movie, and it's incredibly challenging and terrifying, and it can certainly be lethal. You need that edge, partly because *Star Trek* has been so relentlessly parodied over the years.'

*Star Trek Into Darkness* explores the relationship between Kirk and Spock as the 2009 film did, and then of course there is the irritable yet lovable McCoy, who never ceases to mock Spock's logical traits. 'That relationship is the core of what Kirk goes through,' Pine said to *Out*'s Shana Naomi Krochmal. 'The arc and the trajectory of his journey is huge, almost Greek. But it's through his relationship with Spock that he learns the greatest lessons, about loving someone to the point of being able to do away with all rules and regulations and constraints in order to save, protect, and do justice to your friend.'

*Star Trek Into Darkness* explores a different side of Kirk, who was arrogant and self-assured in the first film. He expresses moments of self-doubt and a lack of confidence in the second feature. There is an existential crisis for the captain; should he really be in the captain's chair? Should he be at the helm of Starfleet's most famous ship? It became a challenge for Pine to express those emotions and for Abrams to capture them.

The film is dominated by the many scenes between Kirk and Harrison/Khan. The arguments between Kirk and Harrison are part of the structure of the film. In some scenes the two characters are separated by a glass partition, which symbolises how powerful Harrison is; a separate, untouchable power who plagues Kirk with self-doubt.

'He's a phenomenal one-man weapon of mass destruction,' Cumberbatch said at a Q&A with journalists in London, 'both at close-hand combat and with weaponry and also psychological warfare, he can get you to do his bidding. Even when he's not seemingly in a position to have any kind of power or control… it's a great ride, his character's journey in this film.'

Simon Pegg spoke to Ben Pearson of *Geek Nation* about working on the film: 'I was on the film for five months, and on the first film I was on for about four weeks. So it was great to be there from the beginning and there at the very end. With the first film, each character gets introduced in their own [scene], and Scotty happened to be the last one and it was fun doing that because in the story, you're thinking "Where's Scotty?" and he eventually gets there. As an actor, I came into the shoot to an already existing family of people who were waiting for me. So that was interesting. Being on this one from the very top to the very end, that was great. I love these guys, I love hanging out. They're a great bunch.'

The cast and crew had become good friends throughout the making of the two *Star Trek* films and it was hard not to mess around and joke even though it was counterproductive to the overall aim of making a movie. '...Sometimes it's impossible not to get the giggles,' Pegg admitted to *Collider*'s Steve 'Frosty' Weintraub, 'particularly if J.J. falls victim too. Karl is a terror and the combination of Zach, Chris and I can be lethal. Towards the end of the shoot Chris Pine and I played a gigantic practical joke on the rest of the cast, involving a fictitious anti-radiation treatment called neutron cream. There was a lot of laughing during that period. Chris and I were a bit naughty.'

'Just like the natural progression of any friendship, or friendships, we really do get along quite well,' Pine told the staff of *StarTrek.com*. 'There's just this strong bond that we all share. I guess it speaks to J.J. (Abrams) casting this thing that, above and beyond the acting chops, he cast it well in the sense that we get along. If you're going to put a family on the screen for years to come, you'd better hope that they have a love for one another, and we certainly do.'

'The key to this movie working is, no question, the characters,' Abrams elaborated to *MSN Entertainment*'s James Rocchi. 'And while we are incredibly lucky to have an extraordinary cast playing these roles, I do agree with you that it really is the characters, the sort of archetypes, the dynamic that Roddenberry created that really gives this thing its heart and soul. So we really honour the thing that the original fans loved about the show that I later came to appreciate. But at the same time we wanted to infuse it with a kind of visceral energy and say those characters you love, having those debates, dealing with those sort of moral philosophical dilemmas, they are sort of thrust into an adventure that is a little bit more speedy, a little bit more action adventure, a little bit more intense. And that to me was sort of the balance that every day we're struggling to achieve.'

The marketing campaign was typically clever. Paramount released the first official post in December 2012 and several minutes of the film was shown on IMAX before screenings of *The Hobbit: An Unexpected Journey*, which was released in the United States on 14 December 2012. Rumours circulated amongst genre fans as to Cumberbatch's involvement – would he be the villainous original *Star Trek* foe Khan?

Abrams spoke to *The Daily Telegraph*'s John Hiscock about *Star Trek*'s appeal: 'I wanted to do the fans proud and make sure the story is something that touches people. The goal was to try to tell a story which can be seen and enjoyed if you haven't seen the previous one or know anything about the original series. But having said that, there are those fans of *Star Trek* who are very vocal and like things the way they were – we've all met them and I love and respect them because we wouldn't be doing this if it wasn't for them – but we couldn't make a movie just for those fans.'

The biggest star of the film was probably Cumberbatch, who'd already built up a huge fan base around the world through BBC's *Sherlock* series. 'When I went to Japan for *Star*

*Trek*, the fans were at the airport waiting,' Pine said to *Esquire's* Sanjiv Bhattacharya. 'But they didn't scream until Benedict got off the plane. And I was like, fuck man? What about me?'

Hundreds of people were involved in the making of the film, from caterers to set designers to special effects experts; and it wasn't just the production that concerned multiple staff members but dozens of people were involved in the 3D conversion process, too. Abrams knew that he was not solely responsible for its creation. 'When we did the first movie we never got to really experience the movie with a real audience,' Abrams told *The SCI FI Show*. 'We had a lot of friends and family screenings, we would ask people to come in and watch it, but we didn't have any – and the feeling I have when I think back to that time, how nervous we all were when we showed up and how warm the reception was and how nice it was to watch the movie with a real audience. And it was such a great relief. So part of it is, I feel comfortable just being here again and being able to premiere the movie here. To me, honestly it's not about a number, it's not about critical response, it's just sort of the feeling that people have appreciated and enjoyed the work.'

Abrams envisaged *Star Trek Into Darkness* as a stand-alone film. He strove to make it a much bigger, better and bolder film with more emotional impact and action. It was more character-based than the first film with more plotting but still with lots of battles, chases, fight scenes and action. His vision for the production paid dividends. He learned from his mistakes on the first film, too.

'I know I get a lot of grief for that,' he told *CraveOnline* about his overuse of lens flare on the first film. 'But I'll tell you, there are times when I'm working on a shot, I think, "Oh this would be really cool... with a lens flare." But I know it's too much, and I apologise. I'm so aware of it now. I was showing my wife an early cut of *Star Trek Into Darkness* and there was this one scene where she was literally like, "I just can't see what's going on. I don't understand what that is." I was like, "Yeah, I went too nuts on this."'

'This is how stupid it was,' he continued. 'I actually had to use ILM [Industrial Light & Magic] to remove lens flare in a couple of shots, which is, I know, moronic. But I think admitting you're an addict is the first step towards recovery.'

Abrams had made *Star Trek* hip again. He took a series that was derided by some and seemingly only appealed to a certain type of 'fan' and made it accessible to a wider – and more importantly, younger – audience. Abrams still hadn't seen all ten *Star Trek* films and was hardly a scholar of the series. He felt it was an advantage. '*Star Trek*,' he said to *The Guardian*'s Steve Rose in 2009, 'always felt like a silly, campy thing. I remember appreciating it, but feeling like I didn't get it. I felt it didn't give me a way in. There was a captain, there was this first officer, they were talking a lot about adventures and not having them as much as I would've liked. Maybe I wasn't smart enough, maybe I wasn't old enough.'

One criticism of the film is that it failed to 'boldly go' into space to meet new alien life forms, as the *Star Trek* concept originally envisaged. In fact, it is all set on earth. Taking audiences into the past with the casting of Khan was also a risk. Abrams was aware of these comments but he also wanted to bring a whole new generation of film buffs to the *Star Trek* universe. The film was made for everyone who enjoys a good yarn rather than just trekkers.

Asked if he'd now become a fully-fledged *Star Trek* fan, he told the staff at *StarTrek.com* in 2013: 'Well, it's funny, because even full-fledged *Star Trek* fans are at odds with what it means to be a full-fledged *Star Trek* fan. So, do I love the original series now? Yes. I completely embrace it and get it in a way that I never did before. Do I love what we've been able to do [on the new films] and the work that this group has done? Yes. Have I seen enough episodes of *Deep Space Nin*e and *Voyager* to comment on them? No. I have seen enough to go, "Oh wow, I get it," but I have not seen every episode of every version of every *Star Trek* show.'

Cumberbatch walked away from the film with a positive attitude. '...J.J. is extraordinary,' he told an audience of journalists at a press Q&A in London. 'The whole thing about him is that it is to do with family, from him as a person to him as an artist, and what he creates with the crew and the sense of jeopardy within that first nine minutes, you've kind of got that surmised and, whatever the spectacle, whatever the thrills of 3D and IMAX – of which there are aplenty in this film – you actually care about what happens because of the characters involved. And I think that goes for the atmosphere on set, as well. He demands a lot of you, but God you go there willingly because it's enormous fun and he's such a wonderful person to work for.'

Abrams and his writers managed to keep the plot tightly under-wraps and kept the fans guessing about the villain, though most people assumed it would be Khan. 'The best twists are in movies where you don't know there's a twist, that's why when we all saw *The Sixth Sense* we were shocked,' Lindelof told *Slash Film*'s Germain Lussier. 'You suddenly go like "Oh my god, this movie wasn't even presenting itself that way." So just telling me that "There's a twist in *Iron Man*," I go into the theatre and I'm looking for the twist and within ten minutes if you're looking for it, you can pretty much figure it out and that kind of ruined the movie for me in a lot of ways and it's my own damn fault.'

Even though the studio told the producers to get more material out there so audiences would know what they're going to see, Abrams and his colleagues resisted. In any case, they had previewed nine minutes of the movie and they slowly allowed plot details to be uncovered as the film's release date neared. They wanted the audience to be emotionally involved in the story and characters and not inundate them with too many clips and trailers.

New York film buff and co-founder of the New York Asian Film Festival Daniel Craft – who had been diagnosed with terminal cancer in late 2012 – was given the opportunity to watch an early rough cut of the film when his family members and friends made a plea to the website *Reddit*, which subsequently went viral. Craft's wife, Paige, received a voicemail from Abrams and Lindelof saying a producer would get in touch. The next day, one of the producers turned up at the Crafts' house with a DVD containing a rough cut of the film. Grady Hendrix told *Reddit* in a post: 'At a time when he didn't have a whole lot to look forward to, *Star Trek*, J.J. Abrams, Damon Lindelof, and Bad Robot performed a simple act of kindness for a total stranger and gave Dan something to be excited about for a couple of days. The movie did exactly what movies are supposed to do, it helped him forget about his problems for a couple of hours. It doesn't sound like much, but in this case it was.'

*Star Trek Into Darkness* received its premiere at Event Cinemas in Sydney, Australia, in April 2013 and was released in May. It was a critical and commercial success grossing close to $500 million worldwide. The film earned a staggering $13.5 million on its opening day in North America and total weekend box-office earnings of $84.1 million. It is now the highest grossing *Star Trek* film so far in the franchise. Abrams's buddy Tom Cruise turned up at the Los Angeles premiere to offer his support.

Most critics were pleased with the film and gave it good reviews, reserving praise especially for Cumberbatch's performance. Would he be the next Patrick Stewart, Ian McKellen or Alan Rickman? The film did receive some criticism, notably for Alice Eve's character Carol Marcus (who was in the original series and in *Star Trek II – The Wrath of Khan*) appearing in underwear, which some felt was unnecessary in a *Trek* film. She asks Kirk to turn away while she gets changed, which he promptly does, yet the camera just stays on her, which is rather sleazy. Some noted former *Star Trek* actors and fans also felt that it was a mistake to cast a white Englishman in the role of Khan, who was originally played by the late Mexican actor Ricardo Montalbán.

Andrew Pulver wrote in *The Guardian*: 'There's consequently a palpable air of world-weariness about this *Star Trek*; it's as if Abrams and his writers concluded they couldn't replicate the cockiness and bounce of the first film, and opted instead to allow their characters to grow up a little. Everyone is a little more battered, a little less dewy-eyed. People are unlikely to charge out of the cinema with quite the same level of glee as they did in 2009; but this is certainly an astute, exhilarating concoction.'

'Not all of it works – compared to the opener, the last-reel action is enjoyable rather than jaw-dropping – but there is the sense of a true showman at work,' penned Ian Freer in his *Empire* review. 'Like Lucas, Abrams doesn't care about science-fiction, cold fusion thingamys and transwarp doodahs. He just wants you to have as much as fun as humanly possible.'

Matthew Leyland commented in his *Total Film* review: '*Into Darkness* papers over many of the cracks. There's a whole lot less trans-warp theorising for one thing. A more intriguing baddie than Eric Bana's raving revenge-seeker for another. True, our new nemesis, John Harrison (a menacing, mystery-cloaked Benedict Cumberbatch) also has payback on his devilish mind, but it's…complicated.'

Dave Bradley's 3/5 review in *SFX* was moderately critical. 'Back in 2009, Abrams showed his commitment to a fresh vision by wiping out Vulcan, killing Kirk's father in a heart-wrenching pre-credits scene, and shipping Uhura and Spock,' he wrote. 'Today it's as though he just wants more conservative fans to see how much he 'gets' *Trek*. But does he though? An outmoded attitude to female characters undermines Roddenberry's long history of positive role models (we see Carol Marcus gratuitously stripped to her underwear, and Uhura is repeatedly shown to dote on Spock to the point where her professionalism is questioned) and there's rarely any real sense of peril or consequence – Kirk even bounces back from the dead, a recovery that took Spock Prime another whole film.'

Though the film was a commercial success and received mostly positive reviews, a *Star Trek* convention in Las Vegas voted it the worst *Star Trek* movie; even beating the much derided *Star Trek V – The Final Frontier* (directed by William Shatner) and the franchise's first cinematic foray, *The Motion Picture*.

People who had no prior inclination to watch a *Star Trek* movie went to see *Into Darkness* and perhaps some *Star Trek* fans felt their turf was being invaded by outsiders. Nevertheless, *Into Darkness* is the most successful *Star Trek* movie ever at the box office. Period.

'...It absolutely isn't the worst *Star Trek* movie,' a defensive Pegg told the *Huffington Post*'s Mike Ryan. 'It's asinine, you know? It's ridiculous. And frustrating, as well, because a lot of hard work and love went into that movie, and all J.J. wanted to do was make a film that people really enjoyed. So, to be subject to that level of sort of, like, crass fucking ire, I just say fuck you. Not you, but the people who said that. It's also that thing, as I say, that it hasn't been around long enough. It's the newest one. It's the one people least recognise. If you look back at things you really love, there's a big list: the things that you've got to re-watch and enjoy, they are going to be more up there. The thing that you know the least will be at the bottom. So it might be that, too, you know?'

One thing Abrams knows all too well is that you cannot please everyone all the time. Even his hero Steven Spielberg has had weak moments with some of his blockbuster films such as the second *Jurassic Park* movie *The Lost World* and the fourth *Indiana Jones* film, *Kingdom of the Crystal Skull*. Let's not even mention his failed 1979 John Belushi-led comedy, *1941*. His biggest turkey; it makes *Hook* look like *Citizen Kane*. Abrams and his writers did not change the *Star Trek* universe but they certainly made it a little less predictable. 'We have all been living in this world for the last three years,' Kurtzman told *Geek Monthly Magazine*'s Anthony Pascale. 'So the idea that it is finally going to be exposed to everybody is daunting, but at the same time very exciting. Inevitably there is going to be a group of people that don't like what we did, but hopefully there will be more that do. The one thing I can say for sure is that we all did our homework – not just the two of us but Damon [Lindelof], J.J. [Abrams], and Bryan [Burk] all really saturated ourselves in the world so that we knew that whatever choices we are making, we were informed. For that reason we are feeling confident, but nervous because it is such a big thing we are putting out there.'

After some complaints and hesitations from *Star Trek* zealots Abrams had beaten the odds and made two very successful, very appealing and very entertaining *Star Trek* movies, despite some flaws. Most sequels fail because they either try to remake the first film or the creators assume the audiences are already committed because they know the story, the characters and the history. There have been some successful sequels that have surpassed the original films, notably *The Godfather Part II* and the debate continues as to whether *Aliens* is better than *Alien* or *Terminator 2: Judgement Day* is greater than the first *Terminator* film, but on the whole sequels rarely fare well. A third and final *Star Trek* film would have been a fine goodbye salute to the *Star Trek* franchise from Abrams but he set his sights on something even bigger. So who is going to take over the director's chair?

*Star Trek Into Darkness* does continue to explore moral and social issues as the original 1960s series did. *Into Darkness* sees a terrorist attack threaten the future of Starfleet and in the post 9/11 world terrorism is a major global concern. How far do the authorities have to go on a war against terror? What is acceptable? It remains to be seen where the future films will take the franchise.

It was confirmed in 2013 that Abrams would not direct *Star Trek* three, set to be released in 2016. Rumours circulated around Hollywood that Abrams had had enough of the competing ideas on the franchise merchandise between Paramount and CBS who shared the merchandising rights. It left Bad Robot as 'piggy in the middle'. As a consequence of the merchandise tug-of-war Abrams had to drop his plans for a multi-media *Star Trek* extravaganza that spanned TV, digital entertainment and comic books. 'J.J. just threw up his hands,' an insider told *TheWrap*. 'The message was, "Why set up all this when we'll just be competing against ourselves?" The studio wanted to please Bad Robot, but it was allowing CBS to say yea or nay when it came to what was happening with the *Star Trek* products.'

CBS continued to produce toys and merchandise affiliated with the original *Star Trek* series, which confused new fans, who were unsure of the difference between the Abrams reboot and the original series. Reports suggested that Bad Robot politely asked CBS to stop making merchandise of the original series so Bad Robot and Paramount could concentrate on the reboot with Chris Pine as Kirk. CBS was making around $20 million a year on the merchandise that understandably they didn't give up, though they did curtail plans for an affiliated TV series and online presence based on the original 1960s series. Despite the cross-company complications, Paramount, CBS and Bad Robot did work together to create a game, comic book and novelisation based on *Star Trek Into Darkness*.

Paramount and Bad Robot did not respond to *TheWrap*'s 2013 article 'How the Battle Over *Star Trek* Rights Killed J.J. Abrams' Grand Ambitions'. However, a spokesperson for CBS

Consumer Products issued an anodyne press statement: 'As the merchandising rights holder for *Star Trek*, CBS Consumer Products has ongoing relationships with all our partners, including Paramount. We have worked closely with them for the last five years to create merchandise to enhance the movies and satisfy fans. We are all looking forward to a successful opening of *Into Darkness*.'

Aside from the merchandise wrangling, there is a danger for a filmmaker in becoming too heavily associated with big franchises. It's like an actor becoming typecast. Abrams was aware of this and it was surely the major factor in his moving on.

Orci was still on board as writer of the third film, though Kurtzman had decided to move on. 'I will be involved in the story and in the producing of the movie,' he told staff at *StarTrek.com* in 2013. 'Obviously, it matters very much to me, having been there from the very beginning of this incarnation, the next step is a critical thing. I did not work on two movies in a row to run off and not participate. So, my involvement is real. My involvement is emotional. It's not just the actors I want to make sure are on a solid footing, but it's the characters, too.'

'I would love to do nothing but *Star Trek*,' Orci also admitted to *TrekMovie.com*'s Anthony Pascale. 'However, I am aware that not necessarily being the best thing for *Star Trek*. I would want someone to tap me on the shoulder the minute it is stale. And I hope I have the self-control and will to go "You are right, the best thing for me to do now is make a gracious and easy way for someone to come in and continue on."'

Abrams's decision not to direct the third film left the cast and crew feeling disappointed because they had become a family during the making of the 2009 and 2013 films.

'I'm very disappointed that he won't be directing but I am not worried about *Star Trek*'s future because J.J. and his team are in love with this story,' Kirk actor Chris Pine told *The Daily Telegraph*'s John Hiscock. 'I know that no matter what happens and who is in charge on a day-to-day basis, they will protect and care for it.'

'In terms of a director, I don't know,' Pine told *StarTrek.com* in 2013 during a huge publicity blitz. 'What I am sure of is that J.J. and company have a great respect for *Star Trek*, for the franchise, for the history, for the legacy of it, and for what they've done. I can't see them walking away completely without making sure that whoever takes the helm is going to protect that.'

Abrams has too much invested in *Star Trek* simply to walk. 'J.J. will still be very much involved,' said Pegg to Dave Lewis of *Hitfix*. 'His stamp will still be on it. It'll be interesting to see whoever directs it, what they bring to it as well. It'll be another evolution I think.'

*Star Trek* has given Chris Pine the luxury of choosing which roles he wants to accept. After *Star Trek* Pine moved onto relaunching another big franchise, the Jack Ryan series based on the books by the late Tom Clancy. 'Really, what excites me most is the fact that he's so different from Kirk,' he told *StarTrek.com*'s staff. 'Ryan is the thoughtful, quiet hero. He actually has many more qualities that resemble Spock than anything else. I think he's a character who's more comfortable using his mind and his wits…rather than his fists and his brawn.'

'We've addressed some of the classic characters and we're just about to start our five-year mission,' Pegg pointed out to *The Independent*'s Adam Sherwin about future adventures.

'I'd like to see some new stuff coming up. It would be good to come across some new adversaries and original characters. I think we've established ourselves enough to be able to do that so who knows?'

Abrams continued to show his incredible talent for making successful TV shows alongside his Hollywood film career. He sees the positives of both mediums and chooses to invest time and energy in both. Some of the most exciting stories around the time of the release of *Into Darkness* were on television in both the US and UK, not on the big screen: such high profile shows as *Sherlock*, *Doctor Who* and *Game of Thrones*. TV allows creators to explore stories in depth and there's more scope for development, whereas in films scenes and ideas often end up on the cutting room floor. Hopefully, studios will feel challenged by the recent mainstream success of TV and attempt to push the boundaries of creativity in film by developing new ideas rather than continuing to rehash already existing stories.

And Abrams continued to work in TV with *Alcatraz*, which premiered in 2012. Filmed in Vancouver and San Francisco, *Alcatraz* was created by Elizabeth Sarnoff, Steven Lilien and Bryan Wynbrandt and produced by Bad Robot Productions. The story is set in the infamous prison, which was closed in 1963 owing to unsafe conditions for prisoners and staff (or perhaps simply because of its terrible reputation) and switches eras from the 1960s to present-day San Francisco. The prisoners and guards disappear in 1963 and end up in the modern-day city and are being tracked down by a government agency. *Alcatraz* starred Sam Neill, Sarah Jones, Jorge Garcia and Parminder Nagra. It was cancelled in May 2012 after one season. The series was reasonably well received, though ratings declined considerably throughout the run.

Matt Roush wrote in *TV Guide*: 'The mysteries of the mythology – where were they for the last half-century? Who's pulling their violent strings? – are more compelling than the plodding mechanics of the weekly manhunt.'

Alan Sepinwall wrote on *Hitfix*: 'It's much too generic given Abrams' reputation from *Alias*, *Lost*, the better years of *Fringe* and the *Star Trek* reboot.'

Abrams is a work horse. He's got projects constantly on the go. He treats his career much like an office job; after a day at the Bad Robot offices he will go home around seven p.m. and give the kids a bath and put them to bed, and then have dinner with his wife around half eight. If there is still a lot of work to do on a movie or TV show he will do some editing at home. He has a system set up where he can edit from home and still work with the editors at the Bad Robot editing suite. He's in bed for around midnight ready to wake up at seven a.m. and start the day.

'Part of it, in terms of inspiration,' Abrams told PBS's Tavis Smiley, 'is working with people that actually inspire you. I think it's almost a chemical thing. It sounds obvious and silly, but finding people that make you go ooh, I want to come up with a better idea, because I want to impress that person, I want to make that person laugh....It's a thing that whenever you're playing sports with people who are better than you are, it makes you rise to the occasion. So part of it's that, working with people at Bad Robot, with the studios that we work with, the networks we work with, to try and collaborate with inspiration.'

He served as executive producer of *Revolution*, which premiered in 2012. Abrams does not create all the shows he produces and nor does he take the credit for shows such as *Revolution* – he likes to help other storytellers to bring their ideas to TV. Created by Eric Kripke, responsible for the successful and long-running *Supernatural* TV show, *Revolution* is a post-apocalyptic science-fiction series that follows a group of revolutionaries who confront a dictatorial regime fifteen years after a global blackout that shuts down the world's electricity. *Iron Man* director Jon Favreau directed the pilot episode. Abrams was a fan of the idea as soon as Kripke pitched it to the people at Bad Robot Productions and knew that he wanted to be part of its production.

*Revolution* is a TV romp but it is also something of a cautionary tale. With Facebook, Twitter, Instagram et al, younger people especially are losing important inter-personal skills, the ability to speak to each other. In *Revolution*, technology has gone and people have to learn how to interact with each other in frightening situations without mobile phones and the Internet. It's not a documentary, it's an adventure yarn, but it does offer an interesting perspective on the future and our current over-reliance on technology.

Writing about season one Maureen Ryan said in the *Huffington Post*: 'The clash between the callow and the compelling set off an ongoing debate between the hopeful part of my brain, which wants to like a sci-fi-ish show dreamed up by executive producers J.J. Abrams and Eric Kripke, and the scarred part of my brain, which has been burned dozens of times by genre-flavoured shows that had interesting elements or cast members but also disappointing executions and annoying younger characters.'

'Ambitious setups like this don't always hold up,' Alessandra Stanley wrote in *The New York Times*, 'but *Revolution* has the potential to be a more disciplined *Lost* – not necessarily more plausible but with any luck less preposterous and pretentious.'

*Revolution* stars Billy Burke as Miles Matheson, Tracy Spiridakos as Charlotte 'Charlie' Matheson, Elizabeth Mitchell as Rachel (née Porter) Matheson, Zak Orth as Aaron Pittman, Giancarlo Esposito as Major Tom Neville, J.D. Pardo as Jason Neville, David Lyons as President/General Sebastian 'Bass' Monroe, Stephen Collins as Dr Gene Porter, Daniella Alonso as Nora Clayton, Tim Guinee as Ben Matheson, Graham Rogers as Danny Matheson and Anna Lise Phillips as Maggie Foster.

It was renewed for a second season in April 2013. 'One of the things we learned on *Revolution* is we need to pick up the pace a little bit,' Abrams explained to *SheKnows* about season one. 'Sometimes you think this will be a good slow burn.'

But not a particularly long one. With season two they had plenty of story arcs planned involving love, fun and sex as well as action and intrigue. However, NBC cancelled *Revolution* after two seasons on 9 May 2014.

Abrams also played a TV producer in an episode of the animated comedy *Family Guy*. The episode called 'Ratings Guy' was the second episode of the eleventh season and aired on 7 October 2012 in the States. Peter has ruined TV by manipulating Nielsen feedback and enlists the help of several top producers to put things right. Abrams suggests a show about an alien who goes back in time and meets a koala bear in an eastern European town. Peter tells him to run with it.

What's more Abrams also executive-produced the two sci-fi shows *Believe* and *Almost Human*. *Believe* is a science-fiction series created by Alfonso Cuaron (acclaimed director of *Children of Men* and *Gravity*) and Mark Friedman. Mark Friedman backed away from the series in June 2013, which left Cuaron on board as executive producer alongside Abrams. Friedman was replaced by Dave Erickson who stepped down a few months later and was succeeded by Jonas Pate.

*Believe* is about a young girl with special abilities. She is protected by people who seek the help of an outsider because as she grows older she struggles to control her evolving gifts. The outsider is a wrongfully convicted prisoner who is at first reluctant to take on the role as her protector but the pair develop a special bond. They help others while staying one step ahead of the evil forces that want the girl because of her powers. He later finds out he is the girl's father.

*Believe* stars Johnny Sequoyah as Bo, Jake McLaughlin as Tate, Delroy Lindo as Winter, Kyle MacLachlan as Skouras, Sienna Guillory as Moore, Jami Chung as Channing, Arian Moayed as Corey and Tracy Howe as Sparks. The series was initially part of NBC's development projects in September 2012 and a pilot episode was given the go-ahead in January 2013. The series was placed on the network's production schedule for 2013–2014. NBC cancelled *Believe* on 9 May 2014 after just one season.

*Almost Human* was given the green light by Fox in January 2013 after it appeared as part of their development schedule the previous September. A pilot was planned and a full series was given the go-ahead in May. Executive producer Naren Shankar, who became part of the production team after the pilot, left the series due to creative differences. The show's creator J.H. Wyman continued to run the show.

Human police officers, struggling to protect and serve, create a new policy and team up with androids to protect the streets from violent criminals in the year 2048. Detective John Kennex is not happy with the new policy: two years previously, struggling against a violent criminal gang known as Insyndicate, his partner was killed and Kennex's leg was lost in an explosion after an android partner left them at the scene because their chances of survival were slim. The series stars Karl Urban as Detective John Kennex, Michael Ealy as Dorian, Mink Kelly as Detective Valerie Stahl, Mackenzie Crook as Technician Rudy Lom, Michael Irby as Detective Richard Paul and Lili Taylor as Captain Sandra Maldonado.

'As a kid, I used to love *The Six Million Dollar Man* and I loved the idea of...technology and humanity overlapping,' Abrams explained to NPR's Arun Rath. 'What I loved about this idea that Joel Wyman pitched was that...this synthetic partner was in many ways the partner you would want in a cop car with you. He is the guy who was not only brave and incredibly fit and had all of the information you wanted instantly, but is also someone who is actually compassionate and insightful and thoughtful and someone who would really be, in many ways, more human than the human partner he had.... The title *Almost Human* applies to both of the main characters. These are two characters that are sort of broken. They're sort of both, in various ways, on the scrap heap and they both kind of save each other.'

*Almost Human* poses ethical questions as the lead detective, though he detests robots, is not fully human himself because of his robotic leg. The series is a different take on the cop procedural and it is also totally different from anything else in the Bad Robot canon.

*Fringe* was a huge influence on the writers of the show. Both shows explore how far technology can change the lives of every human. Is science getting out of control? How far is far enough? *Fringe* posed philosophical and ethical questions, as is the aim of *Almost Human*.

Even though Abrams relishes science-fiction stories, he has a fascination with the past, which is why perhaps it's curious that he has not yet delved into Steampunk; a subgenre of science-fiction that blends Victorian aesthetics with futuristic technology.

'I'm obsessed with things that are distinctly analogue,' Abrams revealed to *The Guardian*'s Katie Puckrik. 'We have a letterpress in our office. There's an absolute wonderful imperfection that you get when you do a letterpress, and that is the beauty of it. The time that is put in setting the type and running the press, inking the rollers, all that stuff – that kind of thing is clearly an extreme example. But it's the beauty of the actual investment of time, and the amount of time that goes by lets you consider things that, in a kind of weird osmosis or spiritual way, are somehow implicit in the final product. And that seems to not exist much anymore.'

The creators of *Almost Human* spoke to academics at MIT who study robot ethics, as the stories poses questions about civil rights. It's the whole notion that the more advanced robots become, the more human-like they become. They are thinking beings, so do they have rights? 'I think therefore I am' posited the sixteenth-century French philosopher René Descartes. What is a robot? What is an android? The latter is close to a human but not human, yet they can think. Such philosophical questions have been posed by some of science-fiction's greatest thinkers, the most important of all in this field being the late Isaac Asimov, who created the three laws of robotics: (1) A robot may not injure a human being or, through inaction, allow a human being to come to harm; (2) A robot must obey the orders given to it by human beings, except where such orders would conflict with the First Law; (3) A robot must protect its own existence as long as such protection does not conflict with the First or Second Law.

Abrams has a good knowledge of film history, especially genre films and B-movies. *Blade Runner*, the cult science-fiction film directed by Ridley Scott and based on a novel by Philip K. Dick, the renowned science-fiction writer, was also an influence on *Almost Human* and most certainly *Fringe*, too. *Blade Runner* has probably influenced more science-fiction films since its original 1982 release than any other film. With *Almost Human*, however, the creators did not want such a bleak and dark future as portrayed in Ridley Scott's film. Abrams is more of an optimist and his works do show signs of hope and survival as humanity struggles against itself and what it has created. It's possible to look at Abrams's work and miss the hope when following the struggles of the characters, against technology or humanity. But Abrams's creations always have warmth and humour.

'I mean, the noise you hear after people see something you do – whether it's a TV show or a movie – that always makes you see that thing slightly differently,' Abrams said to *The A.V. Club*'s Noel Murray on the difference between working on TV and film. 'The ability of a television series to make adjustments is something you've got to take advantage of. And test-screening a movie can be helpful too. But the part that can be dangerous is when you take those notes as gospel, instead of taking them with a grain of salt. The key is to use the response as one of the tools in your box, as opposed to using it to determine what you do.'

Reviews of the pilot when it first aired in the US were modest. Some felt it was thematically convoluted but visually impressive. 'If you can look past a few disquieting flaws and get past that odd feeling that you've seen it all before,' said Robert Bianco in *USA Today*, 'you'll find the bones of a potentially entertaining series in *Almost Human*.'

Todd VanDerWerff wrote on *The A. V. Club* website: 'Generic cop heroes aren't always a problem if the show around them boasts other interesting characters or an intriguing premise. *Almost Human* has both, but, sadly, everything else in the show's universe takes more after the [Karl] Urban side of things than the [Michael] Ealy.' (Interestingly, also for *A. V. Club*, he wrote an article in June 2014 called 'Why it's time to stop the anti-spoiler paranoia': 'Anti-spoiler zealots largely ignore craft, privileging plot above all else. But the plot is often the least interesting thing about a movie, TV show, or book.' Maybe he should sit down with Abrams and fight this one out.)

Bad Robot was now juggling three major TV shows after completing the five-year run of *Fringe*. Abrams and his cohorts at Bad Robot each have a role to play but they don't run each show individually. They read the scripts, give notes and ideas and look at edits but no one is running any or all of the shows. They all have their own pet projects but give a helping hand in the other creations.

Abrams talked about the cooperation with Jerry Nunn of Chicago's *GoPride Network*. 'With Joel [Wyman], who worked on *Fringe* for five years, when he pitched me the idea for *Almost*

*Human*, I felt like that little kid that I used to be watching *Six Million Dollar Man* and all excited about the idea of what the show could be…When Eric Kripke pitched *Revolution*, I thought that it would be a really amazing, epic story to tell. It was very ambitious. When Jonah pitched *Person of Interest*, we were having a meeting about a feature. He said, "I have this idea for a TV show" and he pitched *Person of Interest*. The great thing is it's like having friends who are great storytellers who are also running these shows. While we read the scripts, and we give notes, and of course look at edits, and all that kind of stuff, it's not like any one of us is running any or all of these shows. They're all separate endeavours…'

Despite its promising first season and an intriguing central concept, Fox cancelled the show in April 2014 after just one season.

On June 2013 news circulated that through Bad Robot's deal with Warner Bros. Television, Abrams was going to produce Rod Serling's final unproduced script, 'The Stops along the Way'. Details were not confirmed but Bad Robot had secured the rights.

All this prodigious television output was not hindering Abrams's journey on the road to Hollywood domination.

CHAPTER 10

# IN A GALAXY FAR, FAR AWAY...

'...I am still terrified by everything I do, what the reaction will be.'
**J.J. Abrams, *Idol Mag*, 2011**

Disney had officially bought Lucasfilm on 30 October 2012 at a valuation of $4.06 billion, though discussions had begun in May 2011 when Abrams was working on *Star Trek Into Darkness*. Disney, who already owned Marvel and Pixar, announced straightaway that they planned to work on a new *Star Wars* movie for 2015 with proposals for two more films, at least. *Star Wars* creator George Lucas said at the press conference: 'For the past thirty-five years, one of my greatest pleasures has been to see *Star Wars* passed from one generation to the next. I've always believed that *Star Wars* could live beyond me, and I thought it was important to set up the transition during my lifetime.'

Rumours circulated about the director of *Star Wars*. J.J. Abrams had turned down the chance to direct *Star Wars: Episode VII* in 2012. 'It was one of the main reasons I initially said no to *Star Wars*,' he told the BBC's Will Gompertz on the subject of being a director who reboots other people's franchises. 'I thought, "I can't be that guy."'

'There were the very early conversations and I quickly said that because of my loyalty to *Star Trek*, and also just being a fan, I wouldn't even want to be involved in the next version of those things,' Abrams said to *Empire* in late 2012. 'I declined any involvement very early on. I'd rather be in the audience not knowing what was coming, rather than being involved in the minutiae of making them.'

Abrams was working on the second *Star Trek* film and couldn't consider anything else, especially something as huge as *Star Wars*. But as production drew to a close on *Star Trek Into Darkness* he began to think more realistically about the possibility of directing the new *Star Wars* film and spoke to Kathleen Kennedy about it, and even Steven Spielberg, who was very encouraging. Abrams also spoke to his wife and as time went on he became more enthusiastic and confident about the prospect.

'We are absolutely going to make [more] *Star Wars* movies, and we're in the midst of the really fun part of the process, which is we're sitting down with a couple of writers, and we're starting to discuss ideas, and we're starting to talk about what those stories might be,' said Kennedy to *Rolling Stone* in a video interview. 'The main thing is to protect these characters.'

Abrams apparently almost entirely turned down *Star Wars* because of his onerous workload and commitments to other projects. He was planning on making a small film, a comedy-drama. But when push came to shove, how could he turn down this once-in-a-lifetime opportunity?

'If there was any pause on J.J.'s part, it was the same pause everybody has – including myself – stepping into this. Which is, it's daunting,' Kennedy said to *The Hollywood Reporter*. 'We spent a lot of time talking about how meaningful *Star Wars* is and the depth of the mythology that George has created and how we carry that into the next chapter.'

It was announced on 25 January 2013 by The Walt Disney Studios and Lucasfilm that Abrams was going to direct and produce *Star Wars Episode VII*.

*Star Wars* would be more suited to Abrams's vision for a multimedia franchise following the headache of *Star Trek* with the merchandising rights being split between Paramount and Viacom, which had left Bad Robot in the middle. *Star Wars* has more lucrative tie-ins than any other franchise in the world and it has a truly global reach. Abrams is said to have a deal that allows him some kind of casting vote in *Star Wars* merchandise decisions and so he has far more control over *Star Wars* spin-offs than he did with *Star Trek*. Disney's plan for *Star Wars* sounds akin to the vision Abrams had for *Star Trek* which, alas, never happened.

'I knew he loved *Star Wars* so much that my first thought was "Oh my God, my friend is going to get to do what he's always wanted to do,"' Roberto Orci said in an *Associated Press* feature by Jill Lawless. 'On the other hand, I'm a *Star Trek* geek, and I was like, "You traitor!"'

Bryan Burk and Bad Robot Productions would produce the latest instalment in the ever expanding *Star Wars* franchise with Lucasfilm chief Kathleen Kennedy: co-founder of Amblin Entertainment with Steven Spielberg. 'I learned firsthand how incredible and persuasive she is,' Abrams said about Kathleen

Kennedy in an interview with *The Hollywood Reporter*. 'The thing about any pre-existing franchise – I'd sort of done that. But when I met with Kathy, it was suddenly very tantalizing.'

Speculation circulated around Hollywood concerning Abrams's future with Paramount Pictures, the company that had released his previous directed films. Rob Moore, the Vice Chairman of Paramount, confirmed that Abrams would still have a creative hand in the future films in the *Star Trek* and *Mission: Impossible* franchises.

'J.J. has, in his own way, some of the same qualities that I always saw in Steven and George,' said Kathleen Kennedy to *USA Today*. 'What all of these men have is the ability to combine a real seriousness about what they do with a sense of humour. So there's a buoyancy, a lightness, a feeling of aspiration to their storytelling. Of hope.'

'I find that a lot of directors are attracted to the dark side,' she continued. 'That's not Steven or George or J.J. They all can explore darkness, but they're not nihilistic.'

Abrams felt incredibly lucky to be part of a series which he didn't even think was going to come back, let alone be given the chance to direct the first feature in the relaunch of the franchise. Having revivified *Mission: Impossible*, *Star Trek* and now *Star Wars*, the media had begun calling him 'The Rebooter' but he rejected the name, as he told *The Daily Telegraph*'s John Hiscock: 'The last thing anybody wants to be known as is The Rebooter. As a storyteller you have to love the characters and feel the passion that comes with the story. The opportunity to do something cool and to feel in my gut that it could be something special is what excites me.'

With *Star Wars*, he was not replacing one franchise for

another. Bad Robot was always working on multiple projects. When Abrams was directing *Super 8*, *Mission: Impossible – Ghost Protocol* was being produced and *Star Trek Into Darkness* was being prepped. They're one of the busiest production companies in Hollywood.

*Star Trek* and *Star Wars* are two separate universes – different stories, different tones, mood and history with totally different characters. Abrams planned to approach *Star Wars* the same way he had *Star Trek* – from an authentic place where he would make a film that he wanted to see by getting the best out of the stories and the characters.

Whereas *Star Wars* is more rock 'n' roll with it its high-speed space battles and laser fights, *Star Trek* is closer to classical music with slower action scenes, and a strong emphasis on the military chain of command. Movies such as *Iron Man* and *Transformers* owe a huge debt to *Star Wars* because of the sheer relentlessness of the action scenes, the speed at which they move along. *Star Trek* has not had that kind of impact as it is focused more on discovery and the journey itself than action.

Further creative endeavours were announced throughout 2013, though *Star Wars* inevitably dominated the media as far as J.J. Abrams's name was concerned: it was confirmed at the D.I.C.E. Conference that Bad Robot had made a deal with Valve Corporation to produce films based on the video games *Portal* and *Half-Life*. 'It's as real as anything in Hollywood ever gets,' Abrams said at the D.I.C.E. Conference. 'Which is that we are really talking to Valve, we are going to be bringing on a writer, we have a lot of very interesting ideas.'

He added: 'We've had so many meetings and finally got to a point where we said, "We need to start making stuff." And so the ideas that we've had for games, the ideas they've had for turning *Portal* and *Half-Life* into a film, we just decided we actually have to start doing this stuff.'

Another film touted is *Mystery on Fifth Avenue* based on *The New York Times* article written by Penelope Green in June 2008 about an apartment on Fifth Avenue in New York City. When the apartment was renovated the architectural designer Eric Clough incorporated lots of puzzles, riddles and hidden objects into the fabric of the place to amuse the children of the incoming occupants. It is under development by Paramount and Bad Robot Productions. Enough bones on which to build a movie? Time will tell (and the clock is certainly ticking). The film was slated for 2013 completion but no release date has been set at the time of writing.

Whatever happens, 2013 turned out to be one hell of a busy year for J.J. Abrams.

CHAPTER 11

# A NOVEL APPROACH: *S.*

'I love stories where the impossible appears believable, plausible and real.'

**J.J. Abrams, *The New York Times*, 2013**

On 20 October 2013 the novel *S.*, written by Doug Dorst and conceived by Abrams, was published, tearing aside the veil of secrecy which had surrounded the project. A trailer was released by Bad Robot called 'Stranger', which promoted the book. It was yet another example of Abrams's thirst for storytelling and his interest in all types of narrative mediums. 'For me, the fun of something like *S.* was taking something that we all know very well,' Abrams said to *The Guardian*'s Horatia Harrod, 'that incredibly analogue, simple and ubiquitous object, which is the novel, and saying, what would happen if the novel had another dimension to it?'

Abrams had the story in his mind for years before it actually became a novel. It was about fifteen years before the book's publication and Abrams was at Los Angeles airport where he saw a paperback by the late thriller author Robert Ludlum on a bench. He opened it and inside was handwritten: 'To whomever finds this book, please read the book, take it somewhere else and leave it for someone else to find it.' Abrams took the book and kept hold if it. He never left it for anyone else. The idea began a thought process for him – what if someone discovered a book that had notes in, responded to them, and left it back at the same place? Could this spark a conversation?

'It was around the summer of 2009 – they handed me the concept and said: "What kind of story would you tell, given this concept?"' Abrams said to *The New Yorker*'s Joshua Rothman. 'And, first of all, I got really excited, because of the challenge of telling a story in this really restricted form. That really appealed to me as a writer. As far as the substance of the story, I was reading a book on the Shakespeare question at the time, and that sent me over into reading about the B. Traven controversy. I started thinking that, if the notion of a book is central to this idea, what if there were a mystery about its author? It seemed like it would be really, really fun to make up an entire bibliography and history about this writer. From there, it was a small step to deciding that the people who are reading the book should be book geeks themselves.' ('B. Traven' is the pen name of a presumably German author who wrote a dozen novels, among them *The Treasure of the Sierra Madre*, adapted for the screen quite brilliantly by John Houston in 1948. No one knows who he really was; his entire life was a mystery and has led academics, scholars and biographers to dispute the details of his life.)

Dorst is – or rather was until the release of *S.* – best known for his debut novel *Alive in Necropolis*, a paranormal novel about a trainee cop who has to contend with suspects who are both alive and dead. It's a police procedural of sorts as the book has some very realistic police reports and it is Dorst's skill at thinking beyond convention which made him the most appropriate author for Abrams's proposed novel. The idea of mind puzzles and game-playing appealed to Dorst, who agreed immediately to work on the book with Abrams. Dorst got a call one day out of the blue from the Bad Robot offices asking if he'd like to work on such a project with J.J. Abrams.

'I didn't find out that's how it had worked until very recently,' he admitted to *LA Book Review*'s Richard Z. Santos, 'I assumed I was auditioning for the gig. And that probably helped me. They asked me to put together a proposal. "Given this formal conceit, what kind of story would you tell? What would you do with it?" And I thought, well I'm obviously competing for this, I probably won't get it, so I should just design it for maximum fun.'

Abrams had an idea firmly cemented in mind of what he wanted to do and he knew he wanted there to be a love story. He liked the fact that Dorst's proposal did not seem mechanical and calculated. Much of the first year was spent not writing but discussing ideas and characters, themes and story arcs. They also discussed what the book would actually look like and how it would feel. During the discussions Abrams and Dorst built up a friendship and trust and once they had a fair idea of where they were going with the novel, Abrams allowed Dorst time to improvise as much as he needed to. Dorst flew to LA a couple of times from his home in Texas where he teaches at Texas State University, San Marcos. He had a few conference calls with Abrams and worked closely with Lindsey Weber. Dorst is a graduate of the Iowa Writers' Workshop and a former

Wallace Stegner Fellow at Stanford. In addition he has received Fellowships from the Michener-Copernicus Society and the National Endowment for the Arts.

Abrams made it abundantly clear in interviews that Dorst, whom Abrams had met via Bad Robot employee Lindsey Weber after she had read Dorst's book *Alive in Necropolis*, wrote the book based on his idea. '…Working on this project was different from anything I've ever been involved in,' he told *The New York Times*. 'The multi-layered conceit of the thing almost makes it a play interacting with a book. That is, there is the novel itself (*Ship of Theseus*), which stands alone as its own story, and then there are the notes in the margins: a conversation and investigation and mystery and love story between two people, which is both connected to and separate from the central text. Then, there is the editor of the book, who appears in an introduction and in footnotes.'

'…He was adamant the whole way through that I was the writer and that the credit was not to be blurred in any way,' Dorst said to *LA Book Review*'s Richard Z. Santos. 'And he did not have to do that, and he did from the beginning. I respect the hell out of that and appreciate it. He's a good dude. I decided that the best way to approach working with someone who's such a phenomenon, who has so many amazing projects, is just to pretend that's not the case, and say, "Hey, we're making a book. Period." And just focus on the book.'

Dorst found the experience of writing the book to be a trial and error process, as are most creative pursuits. He didn't organise the marginal notes with a whiteboard or anything like that. It was a huge undertaking and a labour of love for the pair.

'My wish list was ridiculously long, but that was part of the fun, too,' Dorst admitted to Christian DuChateau of CNN. 'There were times as I was writing it might occur to me that there would be some sort of exterior piece of information or document that might go with that nicely and I would make a note of it. We didn't really sit down to figure out which ones would serve the story best until later.'

Dorst wrote the foreword and a chapter (with the comments) as they were putting the pitch together for the publishers and then he wrote the rest of *Ship of Theseus* straight through. He'd then put in the comments and made copious notes all through the writing process. It all required a huge amount of concentration and dedication, not to say attention to detail.

'I think that it is a kind of wonderful cocktail of writing of a period,' Abrams said to CNN's Christian DuChateau, 'in a tone that feels really idiosyncratic but then it's got modern-day language and a very current rhythm. While there's an investigation into this author and the conspiracy that swirls around him, it's also a love story, actually more than one love story that develops. It's kind of a wonderful thing to see how it blossoms. I just think Doug truly outdid himself.'

Abrams and Dorst planned the story the way screenwriters work on scripts – they had outlines and pitches to begin with before the earlier chapters were written. Lindsey Weber worked with Dorst before it went to Abrams. Obviously it was a different experience for Abrams – there was no need for casting or filming. The company that designed the book, Melcher Media, did a wonderful job making the finished product look the way it does.

'I knew I wanted *S.*,' Dorst explained to *Geeks of the Galaxy* Podcast, 'the character, to be shanghaied onto this very strange ship that would be a hostile, unpleasant place to be, and it seemed like silence would be the best part of that hostility… So I thought, OK, the crew will not speak to him, it'll be a completely silent ship. And then I thought, well, there has to be something interesting about their silence, so I was like, "All right, let me stitch their mouths shut. That makes me feel creepy." I wasn't really expecting anything like the image that concludes the first trailer that Bad Robot made. It's this figure walking up to the camera, and you actually see this disturbing face that's all sewn up. And, I mean, that freaked me out. I was like, "I wrote the damned thing and this is going to give me nightmares."'

The author of the novel (within the novel) is V.M. Straka who comes right out of the world of Albert Camus and other philosophical writers. College senior Jen and grad student Eric are the two characters who bond over the book and correspond with each other in the margins of Straka's latest novel, *Ship of Theseus*. There are certainly touches of H.P. Lovecraft, Franz Kafka and Vladimir Nabokov. 'I knew I wanted to work with an authorship controversy,' Dorst told *Slate Book Review*. '(I'd been reading about the Shakespeare question, and that had in turn sent me down one of those intoxicating Internet rabbit holes. Well, more than one.) I had a rudimentary sense of who the main characters might be and how Straka might have structured *Ship of Theseus*. J.J. and Lindsey and I talked a lot about how the larger book – *S.* – would work, as well as how the characters might develop.'

In the age of the Internet and instant information Abrams is intrigued by the idea of a sense of anticipation; that something, anything, could happen at any given moment. Abrams is a fan of authors who create concepts that are totally implausible but achieve verisimilitude within the story. Much of his work in TV and film follows this credo. One inspiration was the novel *Jurassic Park* by the late best-selling author Michael Crichton. Abrams and Dorst share a love of Stephen King novels. Abrams's other literary influences include Mark Twain, Graham Greene and H.G. Wells. One other influence was the British supernatural author Dennis Wheatley, whose novels include the occult classic *The Devil Rides Out*. Wheatley would include evidence of the murders in his books and readers would open envelopes to reveal further details about the story. 'There was one I remember called *Who Killed Robert Prentice?* Abrams said to *LA Times*'s Gina McIntyre. 'It had a torn-up photograph in these little wax paper envelopes. As a child, I remember seeing those. That always stayed with me, that idea of getting a book, a packet, that was not just like any other book.'

There's a novel unfolding in the margins of the novel and both novels had to work on their own merits and offer plausible realities. It was important to create a believable world.

'I have no choice but to trust the readers' focus,' Dorst said to Lauren Herstik of *Nerdist*. 'It's a little more demanding of the reader than a lot of what's out there. But we said, "let's not be afraid of that. Let's just tell the story the best we can in the most interesting way it can be told."'

Like much of Abrams's work, the book is a character study rather than a typical genre piece. There is a sense of wonder in the novel, much like the 'hard' science-fiction novels of the golden age produced by authors such as 'The Big Three' of hard SF, Robert Heinlein, Arthur C. Clarke and Isaac Asimov, and Grand Master of SF Robert Silverberg.

'It's an unusual experience,' Dorst explained to Andrew Williams of *Metro* in 2013. 'It's a slip case that contains what looks like an old library book called the *Ship of Theseus*. You open that and discover it has been annotated; two people have written back and forth to each other in the margins. You learn the author of the book is at the centre of a controversy and these two people are investigating his identity and a potentially more dangerous intrigue. Within the book are pieces of ephemera: postcards, maps, letters, artefacts of this investigation.'

The novel itself is a celebration of books – it is fundamentally a love story concerning a book that connects two people; it's also a love letter to books. The idea was that the book would build a connection, a relationship, between two people in a world where individuals are increasingly physically isolated owing to modern technology. The book has handwriting, the kind of personal intimacy that Abrams and Dorst wanted. Interestingly, the handwriting changes as the characters change through the story. Abrams later spoke about the aesthetics of the book to *The New Yorker*'s Joshua Rothman: 'It's intended to be a celebration of the analogue, of the physical object. In this moment of e-mails, and texting, and everything moving into the cloud, in an intangible way, it's intentionally tangible. We wanted to include things you can actually hold in your hand: postcards, Xeroxes, legal-pad pages, pages from the school newspaper, a map on a napkin.'

*S.* is a huge production, much like one of Abrams's films, made to look like an old library book. It includes handwritten letters, postcards, and a code wheel and a map drawn on a napkin; it's a realised novel of some depth and complexity and at the same time a thing of beauty. There is almost inevitably something romantic about a physical book in a digital age.

'We knew from the beginning that the inner novel would have to stand on its own as a work of literature that people are still talking about decades later,' said Dorst to Gina McIntyre of the *LA Times*. 'After we'd committed to it, it did occur to me what I'd gotten myself into. It was about following the story through and taking as many idiosyncratic turns as presented themselves because I was trying to write as this other writer who is known for being an idiosyncratic writer.'

A video was uploaded on YouTube in August 2009 advertising *S.*. It's a black-and-white video featuring a man staggering out of the ocean while a narrator asks 'Who is he?' The video finishes with a close-up of the man whose lips are stitched together. Two-and-a-half million people viewed the video and theories circulated about Abrams's mysterious project. Was it a follow up to *Cloverfield*? Or a trailer for his upcoming TV series *Believe*? Fans did not expect the project to be a novel. It was another ingenious stroke of marketing from Bad Robot Productions. The book was shrouded in so much secrecy that even Pam Brown, the marketing manager for Mulholland Books who published the novel in the States, could not see it. Editor Joshua Kendall was behind Abrams and Dorst all the way. The book was given an initial print run of 200,000 copies and retailed at $35.

'The hardest part was making the time to strictly devote days and days and weeks to editing the book,' Kendall told *Slate Book Review*, 'and given we went through four-and-a-half edits, it was a regular challenge. Running the Mulholland Books imprint, I had to learn to delegate pretty quickly, and luckily I have a terrific staff both in editorial and marketing. As to the editing, as you'll recall I'm a great believer in the very long, comprehensive editorial letter that reframes the conversation of and goals for the book. I saw those letters as a gathering place for all of us.'

The book was mostly well-received, though it did not escape without complaints and criticisms, some fairly vicious.

'Formally, it's as creaky as the knackered old boat on which its hapless protagonist takes passage, and Dorst's talent isn't sufficient to keep incredulity at bay,' Tim Martin wrote in *The Daily Telegraph*. 'He manages to give believable voices to Eric and Jen, the modern-day commentators, but never sells us on the essentially ridiculous thesis that they trade so much information via the book; and the Straka narrative, which tries hard for its sonorous, Conradian tone, comes across inescapably as 21st-century American demotic larded with silly ten-dollar words.'

Mark Lawson in *The Guardian*: 'Although an electronic edition has been released, the book should clearly be experienced in its physical form, which is one of the most staggering feats of book production I have ever seen. Indeed, Abrams's major contribution to the project is to have come up with the antihistorical concept of an analogue interactive book. Such is the suspicion raised in the reader by the book's many tricks that the idea rapidly takes hold that "Doug Dorst" is actually Abrams, making a novel-writing debut under protective cover.'

One reviewer wrote in *The Independent*: 'Fans of *Lost*, Abrams' first television success, will be on familiar ground here. There are endless codes to break, puzzles to unlock, mysteries to solve, and Abrams and Dorst are adept at squeezing every last drop of intrigue out of their set-up. The title *Ship of Theseus* refers to Plutarch's paradox on identity – if a ship has every plank replaced over time, is it still the same ship? These days we know the same thing happens to the cells of our body through death and regeneration, so what makes us who we are, and how much do we change over time?'

'Needless to say, *S.* is a very dense read,' Graeme McMillan wrote in *Wired*. '*Ship of Theseus* alone is a 460-odd page book that could best be described as a Kafka pastiche in which the amnesiac lead undergoes a journey-cum-political metaphor for the industrial revolution and birth of the military-industrial complex, complete with assassinations, ghost pirate ships and potential time travel mixed in for good measure. *S.* the book goes far beyond that, though, with ephemera like newspaper clippings, letters, postcards and photographs scattered throughout. It isn't a difficult read, however.'

However, despite mostly good reviews and a 3.8 star rating on *Goodreads* as well as a heavy marketing campaign, UK sales were not spectacular with just under 20,000 copies sold between October 2013 and the first week of May 2014. Perhaps the paperback version will shift more copies when it is released. In the US *The Hollywood Reporter* claimed that some librarians had banned the book because of the impractical pull-outs, which would make their job a nightmare. (Many publishers have come up with the same 'original' idea – when faced with the awful spectre of the digital world – of making the book a physical object of beauty, rather than a medium. Few have made any money trying it. Though some, probably most, prefer the optimism of Douglas Adams, who told fellow-writer Neil Gaiman why he was so confident the book wasn't on the way out: 'Books are sharks…because sharks have been around for a very long time. There were sharks before there were dinosaurs, and the reason sharks are still in the ocean is that nothing is better at being a shark than a shark.')

Ultimately, what did Abrams want readers to gain from the book?

'I hope they feel like they are opening a door into an experience,' he told *Slate Book Review*, 'into a relationship, into a mystery and investigation, and a whole world that revolves around V.M. Straka, and I think that because the conversations are so funny, and their flirtation is so sweet, and the mystery is so compelling, and the danger is so real, that as you read it you get caught up in the drama of the story. The gimmick of the book is suddenly invisible, and it becomes as real as if you'd actually found this artefact of this love story and this mystery in a university library.'

Regardless of its modest sales, *S.* was another, different expression of Abrams's never-ending desire to narrate. He is a visionary with a thirst to try as many storytelling mediums as possible.

CHAPTER 12

# HOLLYWOOD'S GALACTIC HERO

'Movies can still make disbelief seem beautiful and thrilling, I'd argue.'

**J.J. Abrams, *Time Out Tokyo*, 2011**

Further news surrounding the upcoming *Star Wars* film circulated in the media from 2013 to 2014.

*Toy Story 3* writer Michael Arndt was no longer writing the script, with the baton handed to Abrams and Lawrence Kasdan, who co-wrote *The Empire Strikes Back* and the *Return of the Jedi*, the second and third films in the original *Star Wars* trilogy. Abrams and Kasdan confirmed that they would rewrite Arndt's script.

'I was pleased that there would be new ones,' Kasdan told *IGN*'s Jim Vejvoda, 'that there was a chance to capture some of the spirit of the original trilogy that I'd worked on. I thought there's an audience out there – my grandchildren, lots of original *Star Wars* people – and there always will be. It's only good that we try to do some more great ones.'

'It's funny, because *Star Trek* in some ways, you know,

informed *Star Wars*, and we did *Star Trek*, my love of *Star Wars*, the energy of it, the sort of comedy and rhythm of it, I think affected *Star Trek*,' Abrams said to Tavis Smiley of PBS. 'They're such different worlds, though. The stories, the characters, the universes. One is sort of our future, much more towards science-based in theory, and *Star Wars* is like a fairytale, but it happens to take place in space. They're very different beasts…'

Whereas Abrams was not a *Star Trek* fan, similarly to his pop-culture-obsessed peers, he grew up on *Star Wars*. He didn't feel the same kind of pressure working on *Star Trek* because he wasn't a fan and as such it felt much less of a personal challenge than *Star Wars*, which is something he has loved since childhood and which inspired him to be a filmmaker. His aim is to find a new way to approach the films after the adulation that has been bestowed on the original series and the lukewarm attitude (tending towards hostility and hatred in actual fact) that greeted the prequels released between 1999 and 2005. Getting the script perfect was absolutely paramount.

Abrams spoke to *ChicagoPride Network*'s Jerry Nunn about the script writing process: 'Working with Michael Arndt was a wonderful experience and I couldn't be a bigger fan of his or adore him more. He's a wonderful guy. He was incredibly helpful in the process and working with Larry Kasdan, especially on a *Star Wars* movie, is sort of unbeatable. It became clear that given the timeframe and given the process…working with Larry in this way was going to get us where we needed to be and when we needed to be. That doesn't preclude working with Michael again in the future at all. I couldn't say enough good things about him. He's really, just obviously, one of the smartest guys and one of the best writers around.'

'They're going to be fun.' Kasdan told *IGN*'s Jim Vejvoda. 'J.J. is a great director for the first sequel. Perfect. We're very happy to have him. The writers I've been working with – Michael Arndt, who's going to write the sequel, and Simon Kinberg, who has, like me, been sort of consulting – they're great. I've never really collaborated a lot, and I've never been in a room with a bunch of writers thinking, "Well, what should this thing be?" It's fun. It's really fun. And J.J.'s a writer. Yeah, lovely guy. I'd met him but didn't know him. But now I'm totally enamoured by him. He's really funny and so enthusiastic.'

It was reported in *The Hollywood Reporter* that Kasdan was going to write the scripts for *Episodes VIII* and *IX* with Kinberg, writer of the critically acclaimed *Elysium* and the enjoyable *X-Men: Days of Future Past* but nothing had been officially announced by either Disney or Bad Robot, other than that Kinberg was going to be executive producer on the new animated series *Star Wars Rebels* with Dave Filoni and Greg Weisman.

'I've never seen a level of attention for a movie that isn't in theatres yet as I have for *Star Wars* movies,' said Kinberg, who was inspired to become a film writer and producer after watching *The Empire Strikes Back* and *Raiders of the Lost Ark* as a kid, to *IGN*'s Jim Vejvoda, 'and I understand why, because they are arguably the greatest stories and the biggest cultural benchmark of our time. They're, for our generation, the movies that made many of us want to get into movies in the first place. So there is a level of passion and emotion connected to *Star Wars* that may be greater than other franchises. I try to not worry about speculation about the movies. I just think it's great that there's excitement about the movies. I've worked on movies where you have to generate excitement. This is one where the excitement is built in.'

As well as having Lucas on board as consultant, costume designer Michael Kaplan, who worked with Abrams on the *Star Trek* films, is also involved, as are film editors Maryann Brandon and Mary Jo Markey. Brandon was nominated for an Emmy for her editing work on *Alias* and was also the associate producer of the final season of *Alias*. She edited *Mission: Impossible III*, *Star Trek*, *Super 8* and *Star Trek Into Darkness* for Abrams. Markey's professional relationship with Abrams goes back a little further to *Felicity*. She edited fourteen episodes of *Alias* and was chief editor of *Lost* and also edited *Mission: Impossible III*, *Star Trek*, *Super 8* and *Star Trek Into Darkness*. Her other TV work includes *Breaking News* and *Skins* and the films *Medicine Man* and *The Perks of Being a Wallflower*.

The legendary film composer John Williams confirmed that he would return to compose the score. Several other film crew members were identified on 24 October 2013, including sound designer Ben Burtt, director of photography Daniel Mindel, production designers Rick Carter and Darren Gilford, costume designer Michael Kaplan, special effects supervisor Chris Corbould, re-recording mixer Gary Rydstron, supervising sound editor Matthew Wood, visual effects supervisor Roger Guyett, and executive producers Tommy Harper and Jason McGatlin.

'As a friend to a friend I was ecstatic for him,' actor Chris Pine said to *LA Times*'s *Hero Complex* journalist Rebecca

Keegan. 'If there's one person specifically designed to take care of a project that big, it's J.J., just seeing how he operates on a $200-something-million project like *Star Trek*. I would only be unhappy if he didn't come back and direct the third [*Star Trek* movie]. I don't know what it means for that.'

Spock actor Zachary Quinto also expressed his pleasure to Rebecca Keegan at hearing of Abrams's latest venture into space; this time in the Millennium Falcon (fans hoped!) rather than the Starship Enterprise: 'Knowing J.J., this makes perfect sense. Knowing the legacy he's building for himself, as one of the most accomplished directors of his time, it wasn't surprising. It made me really happy to know that he loves it so much. He's the *Star Wars* guy. He's got all his bases covered. It's the ultimate dream fulfilment.'

'We're very excited to share the official 2015 release date for *Star Wars: Episode VII*, where it will not only anchor the popular holiday filmgoing season but also ensure our extraordinary filmmaking team has the time needed to deliver a sensational picture,' said Alan Horn, chairman of Walt Disney Studios in November 2013.

The 18 December 2015 release date is scheduled so as not to clash with the May 2015 release of the *Avengers* sequel, *Age of Ultron*, from Marvel Studios (directed by Josh Whedon who wrote and directed the massively successful first *Avengers* film). It is part of the third trilogy of *Star Wars* films and the first film since Lucasfilm was bought by Disney studios. George Lucas was announced as creative consultant not only on *Episode VII* but also future *Star Wars* films.

Almost immediately there were lots of rumours surrounding whether Abrams would cast Carrie Fisher, Mark Hamill and

Harrison Ford, the lead stars of the original trilogy. Some reports suggested that the studio had hired personal trainers and nutritionists for Fisher and Hamill to get them back into shape for the role. The studio was apparently happy about Ford's health. Eventually they signed up, more than a year after the rumours started circulating.

'I think he's a great storyteller,' Ford – who starred in Abrams's earlier film *Regarding Henry* – told MTV. 'He's developed an enormous filmmaking skill. I think it's a daunting project, and he's the kind of guy that can take on huge challenges and deliver.'

Aside from the classical Brit actors Alec Guinness and Peter Cushing the original *Star Wars* film relied on unknown actors, and Simon Pegg believes Abrams should do the same with his film, as it creates a more believable world. 'I don't think it would be appropriate for me to be in it, to be honest,' Pegg said to *The Independent*'s Adam Sherwin. 'I think J.J. should cast new faces with no stunt casting. I wouldn't want to be popped out of [enjoyment of] the film by a knowing cameo. I think it would be great to do it properly.'

There had been casting rumours for months with all sorts of wild ideas. Casting calls were held in the UK in September 2013 asking for 'Male, 7 ft. to 7.3 ft. tall with a slim/thin build and upright posture. Not too worked out or too "thick set" especially in the shoulders. Broad facial features would be a bonus', which led to speculation that they were casting for the role of Chewbacca. Original actor Peter Mayhew expressed interest, despite his health issues relating to gigantism. The British Texas-based actor is about seven-foot three-inches (2.21 m) tall.

On 19 November 2013 R2-D2 was confirmed as the first character in the film.

Actors Ewan McGregor (who appeared in the *Star Wars* prequels) *Star Trek* actor Leonard Nimoy and Dwayne 'The Rock' Johnson said they would be interested in appearing in the film during interviews, should they be asked.

Nineteen-year-old actress Saoirse Ronan confirmed on 1 October 2013 that she had auditioned for a role and was not allowed to reveal details of the audition. She later confirmed that she did not get the part. Actor Michael B. Jordan then confirmed on 10 October that he had auditioned for a part.

It was then confirmed in February 2014 that Zac Efron, star of *High School Musical*, had been in talks with Abrams about starring in the new movie. Abrams has to close the gaps between the two generations of *Star Wars* fans – those who grew up on the original series and those who watched the prequels. Of course, there are other fans but it is primarily those two definitive fan bases that Abrams has to start by pleasing; and by casting young, good-looking and popular actors such as Efron he will be opening up the *Star Wars* universe to a whole new legion of fans, just as he did with *Star Trek*.

Reports in February had also suggested that Adam Driver who played the neurotic Adam Sackler of the TV show *Girls* was cast as a Darth Vader-like villain. His co-star Lena Dunham even congratulated him on Twitter ('We're VERY proud of Adam Driver re: *Star Wars*. He's about to rip a hole in da force. Is that a thing? I guess I should see those movies?'), though nothing had been confirmed by Abrams or Lucasfilm.

Further rumours about casting began as it was confirmed

that Abrams had meetings with *Breaking Bad* and *Friday Night Lights* star Jesse Plemons. 'He is one of the actors that we've talked to, yeah,' said Abrams to *Collider*. 'It's not often that I read about actors that I'm going to be meeting. I get to read articles about actors who were going to come in, so I get to see someone and say, "Oh, I read that I was going to see you. It's very nice to see you." It's usually agents talking to people about what's happening. It's just a lot of noise.'

Other less plausible rumours circulated such as that Dame Judi Dench, one of Britain's finest female actors, had been considered for the role of Mon Mothma, a founder of the Rebel Alliance. These rumours had come from *Big Shiny Robot's Full of Sith* podcast and *Latino Review*. Chiwetel Ejiofor, Benedict Cumberbatch, Sullivan Stapleton, Liam McIntyre and Simon Pegg had also been rumoured to appear at some point or another.

'God, there have been so many of them, honestly,' Abrams said to *Collider*. 'I don't know. But, it's amazing to see how many there are. It's really remarkable. But, it's sweet because it shows that there's an interest in this movie that we all obviously know is there. It is an incredible thing to see how many crazy things get thrown out that people then often write commentaries about how happy they are or how disappointed they are about something that's completely false. But, it's a lot of noise, frankly.'

*Star Wars* has a history of using British actors, from Alec Guinness and Peter Cushing in the original series to Liam Neeson and Christopher Lee in the prequels, so it wasn't entirely surprising when in February Gary Oldman revealed during a Sky Movies interview about his role in the *RoboCop* remake that they had spoken to him about the idea of appearing in *Episode VII*. '...You know, I'm more cynical about it now. I'll believe it when I'm on the plane home. The deal isn't done, but yeah, they've inquired. I mean *Planet of the Apes*, *Harry Potter*, *Batman* and *Star Wars*...bloody hell!' Anyway, the British Kenny Baker was back. And the Swede Max von Sydow would be providing some Northern European gravitas.

At the time of writing no plot details had been announced about the new film though it is known that Lucas handed over story treatments to Disney chairman Bob Iger around the time Lucasfilm was sold to Disney. Lucas also had treatments for *Episodes VIII* and *IX*. Fans were left frustrated with the lack of confirmed news on the film's casting, let alone the plot details.

Abrams prefers to keep his productions under wraps and to create as much mystery around them as possible. 'Like with *Cloverfield*, the whole idea with the marketing and the quick release was for people to have an experience as it happened, instead of pre-experiencing it by reading all about it,' he explained to *The A.V. Club*'s Noel Murray. 'But I feel like with *Fringe*, the mandate is to try to do something week-to-week that's a procedural like *CSI*, but a *skewed* procedural, that's as creepy as humanly possible. While with *Lost*, on the one hand, it is a show that seems to duck answering questions. At the end of the pilot, you have Charlie asking "Where are we?" and that's something the audience still wants to find out. But week-to-week, that show answers a lot of questions, just not always the ones people feel are the ones that matter.'

Plot rumours contend *Episode VII* will be set around twenty years after the *Return of the Jedi*; R2-D2 and C-3P0 would be the only characters to feature in all nine films; the trilogy would see the rebuilding of the Republic; Luke Skywalker, Han Solo and Princess Leia would appear in their sixties or seventies; there'd be three generations of the said key characters; there'd be a love story and that there'd be moral and philosophical themes. All hearsay.

Abrams spoke to *The Times*'s Rhys Blakely in 2013 about his interest in the *Star Wars* mythology: 'If you watch the first movie, you don't actually know exactly what the Empire is trying to do. They're going to rule by fear – but you don't know what their endgame is. You don't know what Leia is princess of. You don't yet understand who Jabba the Hutt is, even though there is a reference to him. You don't know that Vader is Luke's father, Leia is his sister – but the possibility is all there. The beauty of that movie was that it was an unfamiliar world, and yet you wanted to see it expand and to see where it went.'

With *Star Wars Episode VII* Abrams is surely set to become one of the most successful Hollywood directors in history standing alongside such giants as Steven Spielberg, George Lucas and James Cameron.

'*Star Wars* is in every way a different animal,' Abrams said to *The Guardian*'s Horatia Harrod. 'It's always been a more open, fan-engaged universe than I've been used to, so I'm sure there'll be some sort of compromise. But it feels to me like there's a purity in not knowing every little thing.'

One frustrating aspect of working on the new *Star Wars* film for Abrams was moving production over to England where the original trilogy had been filmed. Abrams had filmed his previous work in Los Angeles (despite the higher costs) so that he did not have to leave the family home in Pacific Palisades, LA.

Representatives of Lucasfilm met with George Osborne, the Chancellor of the Exchequer, to agree to produce *Episode VII* in the UK at Pinewood Studios. The script was planned to be finalised in January 2014 with filming due to begin in the spring, which was confirmed by Walt Disney Studios chairman Alan Horn on 2 April. Some filming would also take part in the US at the Bad Robot facility in LA and in the Middle East.

The idea was to have the film reflect the look and feel of the original films as far as possible, which meant that cinematographer Daniel Mindel – who'd worked on previous Abrams films, *Mission: Impossible III*, *Star Trek* and *Star Trek Into Darkness* – would shoot in 35mm film and would use release locations and scale models rather than CGI.

Abrams is a huge fan of the advancement of modern technology, which has become essential in bringing science-fiction and fantasy stories to the big screen. And yet there is a downside, as he explained to Jessica Furseth of *Idol Mag*: 'And I think it goes far beyond just film. There is now a kind of instant information, instant purchase, instant understanding that is so counter-intuitive and lacking in experience. Think about [when you had] to get in your car or on your bike and go to the store, walking through the aisles, hearing the other music and finding the album and going to buy it. Then you pay and you're meeting the person who's working there... There's a whole investment into that and when you get home you make sure you listen to that song or the whole album because you've just [done all this].'

Abrams said that he chose not to film it in IMAX because it is a very loud camera and there's only so much film that can be placed in it, so it's difficult to film intimate scenes. IMAX cameras often break down, thus disrupting filming.

'I love technology,' said Abrams to *Den of Geek*'s Luke Savage. 'I think that what we're able to do now in terms of effects in film is amazing. However, my favourite kind of visual effects involve model-making and miniatures that used to be used in movies and are rarely used now because they construct everything in a computer.'

Most franchises are rebooted so the studio can sell already existing merchandise to already existing audiences. Abrams is always more interested in creating something fresh that does not already pre-exist – but he could not turn down the chance to be a part of both *Star Trek* and *Star Wars*. So some kind of artistic tension already exists before the cameras roll.

Abrams was asked by *Empire* magazine if his love of *Star Wars* would have an effect on his vision for the film. Could he stay objective and make an honest film rather than a sort of fan tribute? 'I don't know because we're just getting started. So it's a great question that I hope I'll have a good answer to when I know what the answer is. There are infinitely more questions than answers right now, but to me, they're not that dissimilar. Though I came at these both from very different places, where they both meet is a place of "Ooh, that's really exciting." And even though I was never a *Star Trek* fan, I felt like there was a version of it that would make me excited, that I would think "that's cool, that feels right, I actually would want to see that."...How we were going to get there, what the choices were going to be, who was going to be in it – all of those things I knew would have to be figured out, but it was all based on a foundation of this indescribable, guttural passion for something that could be. It's a similar feeling that I have with *Star Wars.* I feel like I can identify a hunger for what I would want to see again and that is an incredibly exciting place to begin a project. The movies, the worlds could not be more different but that feeling that there's something amazing here is the thing that they share.'

Abrams is a Spielbergian filmmaker who makes movies for large audiences and at the same time has a deep personal connection to his stories. Some of those stories connect with audiences, some don't. It's the nature of the beast. Abrams is a certainly a film geek but not in the obvious pop culture reference way that Quentin Tarantino is, or the hip, self-referential style of Kevin Smith or the über-sophisticated heavy duty way of Christopher Nolan.

Abrams has not become a mouthpiece or cheerleader for a generation of filmmakers but he is often asked for tips on how to make a movie. 'I would say the following thing,' he said to *The SCI FI Show*, 'which is that when I was a kid this kind of question was a tricky answer because, you know, I guess the best thing you could say is keep writing and keep trying to write a great script. Now you can just make your movie. That's the thing that's so crazy. There are so many opportunities, tools and resources that it's unbelievable. The thing that you're recording this conversation with can be used to make a movie. No, of course it's not a Canon 5D or Red Cam but the fact is most everyone has access to some form of moviemaking so the beautiful answer now is – make your movie. There's nothing stopping you. You could actually create the thing using off-the-shelf software and hardware. And I understand that not everyone can afford that equipment but it's readily available. So whether it's about renting or borrowing or owning and anyone it seems has within their reach the tools to access their movie. So I would say make your movie and distribute it to the world the second you're finished with it.'

Mystery has always surrounded Abrams's work before it is released. 'I will sit in a meeting before a movie with 80-some people, heads of departments, and literally say that all I ask is that we preserve the experience for the viewer,' Abrams said to *Entertainment Weekly TV*'s James Hibberd. 'Every choice we make, every costume fitting, every pad of makeup, every set that's built – all that stuff becomes less magical if it's discussed and revealed and pictures are posted online. I just want to make sure that when somebody sees something in a movie they didn't watch a 60-minute behind-the-scene that came out two months before.'

Abrams dislikes nothing more than going to see a film after having watched the trailer and being disappointed that all the best bits of the movie were in it. It's almost like having a second viewing. Abrams, along with his cast and crew, work hard to limit the script's distribution. Obviously there is no guarantee that the experience will be a thrill but Abrams gives it his best shot. For Abrams, watching a movie for the first time should be a surprise. He tries not to force-feed the audience – especially before the meal!

As a writer, producer and director, which role does he enjoy the most? 'Directing's the best part,' he said to *The A.V. Club*'s Noel Murray. 'Whenever I've directed something, there's this feeling of demand and focus that I like. And secondly, it means that you've gotten through all the writing stuff, and the producing stuff, and casting, and prep, and all those stages that are seemingly endless. So directing is sort of the reward for all the work you put in before. And then there's the editing, which is another amazing stage of the process. It's incredible the moments you can create.'

Abrams has become a massively popular name in the world of science-fiction and fantasy, but it's the stories he cherishes rather than the genre. He is currently at the top of his game and one of the key players in Hollywood. As a tech savvy filmmaker with a passion for the history of film and a deep understanding of the needs of his audiences he has become the Spielberg of his generation. Naturally he won't get it right every time. Even Spielberg has directed some questionable films (there's the forgettable World War II box office bomb comedy *1941*, which was released in 1979, 1991's risible *Hook* and more recently the painful *War Horse*, released in 2011) but Spielberg does hit the right note with at least one major film every decade. Much like Spielberg, Abrams wants to move from high-tech summer blockbuster movies to films with more emotional meaning and content yet still connect with the audience as he did with *Super 8*.

A filmmaker such as Michael Bay, probably one of the most derided yet successful directors currently working in Hollywood, creates dumbed down action movies that are often blasted by critics and hit pay dirt (*Transformers*, *Pearl Harbor*); but Abrams concentrates on character and story before he even begins to think about special effects. There are certainly some filmmakers who could learn a thing or two from his uncanny knack of balancing story with effects. Of course at the time of writing it remains to be seen how critics – and more importantly fans – will greet *Star Wars Episode VII* but there's no question that Abrams will do justice to the franchise, especially after George Lucas himself destroyed the hopes and dreams of a generation of fans with the risible *Star Wars Episode I: The Phantom Menace*. Its sequels were marginally better yet still pitifully weak. Lucas is an exceptional producer but he's no writer.

'What will he bring to the franchise? Everything that was missing from the last three,' Pegg told *Total Film* on their Future 100 issue. 'That's what he did to *Star Trek*, really – invigorate it with a little bit of *Star Wars* magic. He switched it from science-fiction to science-fantasy.'

Pegg continued: 'And I think if anyone can pull [*Star Wars*] out of the mire, it's J.J. He'll bring the fun back. Lucas seemed to misread what made the first ones great, and concentrate on things that people didn't really care about, or wilfully ignore the things that people cared about. Whereas J.J. will embrace them all.'

Having said that, despite the critical attacks on the prequel *Star Wars* and the subsequent *Clone Wars* series, they did help to build an entire new (and young!) generation of *Star Wars* fans.

'The truth is, to be lucky enough to get to work on shows at all, let alone shows that you really care about or interest you,' Abrams told Debbie Chang of *BuddyTV*, 'it's a thrill and an honour. Doing *Star Trek*, that really is science-fiction. On *Lost*, you can kind of argue it was a science-fiction show, but we weren't open about that at the beginning. And then *Alias* had a sci-fi bent from the beginning. *Star Trek* is *Star Trek*, you know what I mean? I don't regard the genre as much as I like stories that are often just a little bit off-centre or weirder. That usually means some version of science-fiction.'

The beauty of Abrams's films is that he wants to take the audience back to that sense of wonder that has been lacking in Hollywood films for quite some time. It's the idea that something extraordinary and profound can happen to ordinary people that creates a connection between the characters onscreen and the people watching the film.

It was the poet Coleridge who first used the phrase 'willing suspension of disbelief' way back in 1817, when discussing what a writer of fiction can sometimes evoke in his readers. The trick is the same today: movies should make the viewer suspend disbelief and make the impossible seem possible. And he or she will do so willingly, if the storyteller is good enough.

*Star Wars* was not the only reason why Abrams made the press in early 2014.

In February Abrams had attended a State Dinner at the White House with senior advisor Valerie Jarrett who shared it on Twitter: 'Shout out to all my #trekkies! Great to meet the talented J.J. Abrams at the @WhiteHouse today. pic.twitter.com/PJvFcbuqlH— Valerie Jarrett (@vj44) February 12, 2014.'

Abrams, a Democrat who had donated to the party, also attended the State Dinner on the south lawn of the White House in honour of French President Francois Hollande.

In March he splashed out a staggering $14.5 million on 8,030-square-foot Connecticut Traditional Estate in the posh

Pacific Palisades area of Los Angeles. The two-storey mansion is relatively new, having been built in 1995 and proved the perfect family home for Abrams, his public relations executive wife Katie McGrath – who used to work on Capitol Hill under Ted Kennedy – and their three children: sons August and Henry and daughter Gracie. It hardly made a dent in his estimated fortune of $95 million, which is surely set to grow after the release of *Star Wars*.

As 2014 progressed it was confirmed that a script for *Star Wars Episode VII* had been completed and that casting was being arranged for filming to begin in the UK in May. On 29 April Lucasfilm announced cast details. As mentioned earlier, the film was to include the original actors Mark Hamill, Harrison Ford, Carrie Fisher, Anthony Daniels, Peter Mayhew, and Kenny Baker with Max Von Sydow, Andy Serkis, John Boyega, Daisy Ridley, Adam Driver and Oscar Isaac. 'We are so excited to finally share the cast of *Star Wars: Episode VII*. It is both thrilling and surreal to watch the beloved original cast and these brilliant new performers come together to bring this world to life, once again.' Abrams announced. 'We start shooting in a couple of weeks, and everyone is doing their best to make the fans proud.'

Thousands of fans had turned up for open auditions in 2013 but then in May 2014 Abrams gave hopefuls one last chance to appear in the forthcoming film. One person could win the chance to get dressed up in a costume and make-up and be part of the film. Fans had to donate $10 to the Force for Change campaign in aid of Unicef. Disney itself donated $1 million to this cause. The campaign ran from 21 May to 18 July and the lucky winner would also get an all-expenses-paid trip to London and the full behind-the-scenes VIP treatment.

In a video message to fans, released on 21 May, Abrams said: 'The *Star Wars* fans are some of the most passionate and committed folks around the globe. We're thrilled to offer a chance to come behind the scenes as our VIP guests and be in *Star Wars: Episode VII.* We're even more excited that by participating in this campaign, *Star Wars* fans will be helping children around the world through our collaboration with Unicef Innovation Labs and projects.'

The foundation's chief, Christopher Fabian, said: 'Unicef works in over 190 countries and territories to help the world's most vulnerable children and young people identify solutions and create change. We work together with the greatest technologists and designers of our time to create open-source solutions that help millions of people. The support from *Star Wars: Force For Change* will help to bind these innovators together on a mission to solve the world's most pressing problems, and create a better future.'

It was revealed that Abrams had penned a hand-written motivational letter to the cast and crew as filming began in Abu Dhabi in May. The note read: 'Dearest cast and crew, what an honour it is to work beside all of you on *Star Wars Ep. VII*. I can't thank you enough, for all work past and future. Let's take good care of not just ourselves, but of each other. Amazing, but true: the world awaits this film. Let's give 'em something great. XO JJ'

In June, further cast details were announced. Gwendoline Christie, best known as Brienne of Tarth in *Game of Thrones*, joined the cast as did Lupita Nyong'o, the Oscar-winning actress of *12 Years a Slave*.

One person who was glad not to direct the new *Star Wars* film was George Lucas, who turned seventy in May. He'd taken a lot of criticism for the prequels, which he wrote and directed. 'I get to be a fan now…and I sort of look forward to it,' Lucas said to *Rolling Stone*. 'It's a lot more fun.'

What was Abrams up against? The original *Star Wars* trilogy is beloved by a generation. Lucas wrote and directed the first instalment, *A New Hope*, but handed over the reins for its sequels *The Empire Strikes Back* and *Return of the Jedi*. *The Empire Strikes Back* is often referred to as the deepest, most meaningful and best film of the original three; it was directed by Irvin Kershner and scripted by noted author and screenwriter Leigh Brackett and by Lawrence Kasden.

However, when Lucas revisited *Star Wars* (there were spin-off novels, comics, animated series and the dreaded Ewoks movies to keep fans happen in the interim) in the 1990s for the three prequels, which he wrote and directed himself, the results were less than masterpieces, though box-office receipts were predictably high. *Episode I – The Phantom Menace* was panned by critics and most *Star Wars* fans were left feeling let down. *Attack of the Clones* was only marginally better and while *Revenge of the Sith* had some more effective moments than its two sister films, the prequels did not live up to expectations – but then again, expectations were so high, how could they?

While many original *Star Wars* fans loathed the prequels, the young generations adored them and so along came further *Star Wars* spin-offs; notably *The Clone Wars* films and TV series. The *Star Wars* prequels have been the source of much mockery in the media with some of the lines sounding like corny spoofs of the original films. The prequels seemed to be solely about special effects with no story. Lucas, nevertheless, is a brilliant producer with a powerful imagination, despite his shortcomings, and with Abrams at the helm, only a masterpiece this time around will suffice.

'I don't hate *Star Wars.*' Pegg, who made a famous skit of the *Star Wars* prequels in his cult TV show *Spaced*, told *Huffington Post*'s Mike Ryan. 'I love *Star Wars. Star Wars* is an incredibly formative film for me as a human being and formed so much of who I am. It encouraged a love of classical music in me, because of the score. It encouraged literature and language and my imagination. It formed who I was as a child and it was something that I was incredibly passionate about. The prequels I didn't like at all, because they felt contrary to everything that made the first films great. When I was a kid, I was very protective of *Star Wars*. When *The Black Hole* came out, some kids were going on that it was better than *Star Wars*, I said, "No, it fucking isn't!" It upset me that they would say that.'

Who knows what the reaction will be to Abrams's *Star Wars* film and what the follow-up films will be like? It is likely that Abrams will follow a similar pattern as Spielberg and make smaller films, though Spielberg didn't always get it right. Throughout the 1980s some critics complained that Spielberg was making premeditated attempts to win an Oscar with the likes of *The Colour Purple* and *Empire of the Sun*. (Though why such an ambition should be seen as so reprehensible is difficult to explain.) He finally bagged the Best Director for 1994's *Schindler's List* and a second Oscar for *Saving Private Ryan* in 1999.

Abrams knows about technology, he loves props and film sets as well as special effects but he is also focused on characters and story. Having made such 'big' films – big as in expensive, big in audience appeal – can he make a smaller, more 'meaningful' film? Can he make a comedy where Spielberg failed with *1941* or can he make a war film where George Lucas failed with *Red Tails*?

J.J. Abrams had by now not only become the busiest, most sought-after director in Hollywood, but also one of the most successful. Unlike some of his peers such as Michael Bay, Abrams had also achieved critical acclaim. Though he has yet to make a bona-fide cinematic masterpiece that will stand the test of time and win over the critics, Abrams is well on his way to becoming one of the big screen's most important filmmakers. His films are not perfect. Somewhat ironically, many consider that the best film he has been involved in to-date is *Cloverfield*, which was directed by his buddy Matt Reeves, but there is much to admire about each of his directorial outings – *Mission: Impossible III*, *Super 8*, *Star Trek* and *Star Trek Into Darkness* and hopefully *Star Wars Episode VII*.

Abrams's TV work is often exemplary, though the series can often start off sluggish and become convoluted and bloated. Rather like a first-time novelist, Abrams can be accused of attempting to cram too many ideas into one product. The best filmmakers learn from their mistakes and should by rights become better directors. While Abrams has yet to direct a bad film, he has also yet to progress beyond being a blockbuster director as opposed to so-called serious filmmakers such as Spike Jonze or Paul T Anderson. All these terms – 'progress', 'blockbuster', 'serious' – are of course pretty slippy, hard to get a handle on. Is Hitchcock's *Psycho* a 'blockbuster'? Well it only cost $800,000 but it's the most profitable black-and-white sound film ever made, so is it? *Esquire* described it as 'merely one of those television shows padded out to two hours' – not a 'serious' movie then?

Much of Abrams's work can be seen as paying tribute to his heroes – *Fringe* is evidently his bow to Rod Serling, whose TV series *The Twilight Zone* so inspired the young Abrams. *Mission: Impossible III* is his *Indiana Jones*-style adventure yarn with a dashing action hero at centre stage in Ethan Hunt. *Super 8* is Abrams's nostalgic homage to Spielberg and the Amblin Entertainment movies of the 1980s. *Cloverfield* is a take on the 1950s monster B-movie; he loved those old black-and-white apocalyptic B-movies while he was growing up. *Star Wars* is obviously something he, like many of his peers, considers to be the Holy Grail of blockbuster movies. Probably every director in Hollywood would love to get the opportunity to direct a *Star Wars* movie. It can be facile to compare Abrams with Spielberg but the comparison is too obvious to ignore. It took a while for Spielberg to make films that were not just about making money during the summer holidays and it seems to be taking a while for Abrams to follow suit.

Bad Robot had become its own self-contained world. It became involved in a diversity fellowship program which gave the chance to young filmmakers – film graduates and other aspiring filmmakers as well – to make a film. They picked two directors a year to make their own films. The folks at Bad Robot set them up with heads of departments and arrange interviews to get their films cast and distributed, etc. The one thing that is essential in the filmmaking industry, as in most industries in actual fact, is contacts – who you know and who you can go to for advice and guidance. Bad Robot became a family, welcoming new creative people into their world. They had the fellowship set up for two years and had seen some great work by some very interesting filmmakers. They'd immersed themselves in other charities too, including the Children's Defense Fund. With her background in politics and public relations, Katie McGrath, J.J.'s wife, was instrumental in bringing contacts to Bad Robot and involving them in worthy causes.

With so many productions on the go one might claim J.J. Abrams to be something of a workaholic, but similarly to Spielberg, who is married to actress Kate Capshaw and has seven children from his first marriage to Amy Irving, he has learned to balance everything – his work commitments and his family life. Abrams's mother died in 2012 and he had learned a lot from her about how to be a good parent.

'I think that the key is, and I'm more grateful for this than anything, is that Katie really does help remind me when I'm just getting way too caught up in my own stuff,' Abrams said to PBS TV's Tavis Smiley on the subject of balancing work and home, 'or when I'm taking things way too seriously or when I'm spending too much time. She never says, "Don't do this or do that," she's literally the one who just says, "Do what you want, but this is what I need."...and I'll kind of be like – like I know what that means. It's just I've gone off the rails a little bit. So I feel like how do you balance it, I don't know if balance is the thing. Frankly, I think that you don't even want to balance. You want it to be imbalanced on the side of what really matters.'

The cast details of *Star Wars* overshadowed the news that Abrams's TV shows *Almost Human*, *Believe* and *Revolution* had been cancelled, which prompted TV pundits to question whether his dominance on TV was coming to an end. Alice Vincent, an entertainment writer at *The Daily Telegraph*, penned an article with the headline 'Has JJ Abrams bitten off more than he can chew?' Cancelling TV shows sometimes seems to be an arbitrary process in the US. Many well-written TV shows have fallen by the wayside and been cancelled over the years. Abrams only had one TV show still broadcasting, the increasingly excellent *Person of Interest*, which was renewed for season four in March 2014.

*Star Wars* was taking up so much of his time that he had handed over the reins to *Star Trek 3* to writer Roberto Orci, which would mark the writer's directorial debut. The script was written by Orci, alongside J.D Payne and Patrick McKay. Orci had recently parted company on big screen features with his long-term writing partner Alex Kurtzman who was working on *Venom* for Sony Pictures and was also involved in the Universal reboot of *The Mummy*, which he's producing with Orci and Sean Daniel.

After the completion and release of *Star Wars* perhaps Abrams should follow a different path of filmmaking and surprise his fans and critics with something altogether different, as Joss Whedon did with his 2013 adaptation of Shakespeare's *Much Ado About Nothing*, which was set entirely in his house. After all, such an endeavour was Abrams's intention after the release of the *Star Trek* sequel, but his fan-boy personality won out as soon as the Millennium Falcon came calling, and potential smaller projects were put to one side.

'Being able to take the ideas that occur to me and not let them vanish,' Abrams said to *Wired*'s Jennifer Hillner on the joys of being a movie director in Hollywood, 'to go to the set of something that was in my head. It's a total narcissistic joy to have some private little pleasure, through a lucky stream of events, become tangible, so that you can actually walk on it and touch it. It's cool to bring something to life, whether it's a song or a video. But to do it and have it embraced by millions of people all over the world, like *Lost* – that's insane.'

The history of cinema is littered with salutary tales of woe, whether it be the tortuous process of *Apocalypse Now*, the arduous grind of a Stanley Kubrick production or even the nightmare of *Star Wars*, which ultimately dissuaded George Lucas from directing a film for over two decades and opting for the producer's seat instead. Nevertheless, Abrams is a man who gets his films delivered on time and under budget, which is rare in Tinseltown. It's another reason why he has become Hollywood's Golden Boy in recent years. Paramount are lucky to have him; Disney, luckier, still.

However, after the 2008 economic crash and the recent global recession Hollywood is facing a crisis, not just financially but creatively. There are too many remakes, too many poorly scripted films and more importantly studios have been hit by streaming and downloading where people can watch a film for free online rather than visit their local cinema. If ticket sales and admissions go down, then cinemas close. The windows between releasing a film at the cinema and bringing it out on DVD are becoming increasingly narrow to combat pirates. 'It used to be, when I first started making movies it was really cool, my movies stayed in theatres for one year,' Spielberg said in 2013 at a panel consisting of George Lucas and Microsoft's president of interactive entertainment Don Mattrick, held at the University of Southern California. 'If it was a hit, it was a year-long. *Raiders* [*of the Lost Ark*] was in theatres for a year. *E.T.* was in a theatre for a year and four months...That was an amazing situation, back then.'

As far as America is concerned, the best quality writing in recent years is on television with shows such as *The Wire*, *The Sopranos*, *House of Cards*, *Breaking Bad*, *Mad Men* and *True Detective*. Creative people who want to push the boundaries and don't want to face the reactionary nature of Hollywood – and even its occasional bigotry and ignorance – are turning to cable TV networks such as HBO, as evidenced by *Behind the Candelabra*, a film about the life of Liberace, directed by Steven Soderbergh and starring Michael Douglas and Matt Damon. It was turned down by Hollywood for being 'too gay'. Seasoned actors such as Glenn Close, Kevin Bacon and Kiefer Sutherland have turned to TV because of the alleged ageism that exists in Hollywood.

3D pushes the price of a ticket up and film fans are not daft; they know that most films only have one or two actual 3D scenes in them. Going to the cinema is becoming increasingly like going to a sporting event where you pay top dollar for 'an experience'.

'The movie business is changing at an amazing rate,' Kathleen Kennedy told *USA Today*. 'So to have an intellectual property like *Star Wars* and now be inside a company like Disney, I get to have a seat at the table where we talk about the globalisation of the business, new markets, new audiences and new platforms. I'm just incredibly curious about it all.'

Where does this leave filmmakers like J.J. Abrams?

He will continue to focus on story and character before he invests in the rest of a film and as *Star Wars* will no doubt attest, he has ideas for a major global digital and multi-media platform that will possibly change the way films are made, shown and exploited around the world.

Abrams looks set to dominate the second half of the 2015 film market as the fifth instalment of *Mission: Impossible*, which Abrams is producing, is scheduled to be released on Christmas Day, just a week after *Star Wars – Episode VII* opens on 18 December. *Mission: Impossible – Rogue Nation* is written by Drew Pearce (*Iron Man 3*) and will be directed by Christopher McQuarrie (*Jack Reacher*). The series has been riding high since Abrams's involvement with the third and fourth films. At the time of writing no plot details had been announced.

When asked about his celebrity status, and if he gets attention from women (though he has been happily married for seventeen years and has three children) Abrams told *Playboy* in the May 2013 issue: 'What I usually get isn't a sexual thing. It's usually some dude with hair too long in the back giving me a Vulcan salute or, more recently, saying, "May the force be with you." I haven't gotten a lot of the more appealing versions...'

It is quite possible that 2015 will make Abrams a household name. If the films don't clinch it, an announcement by Steven Spielberg in December would be a slam dunk: 'I am your father.'

# CREDITS

FILMS

**As director:**
*Mission: Impossible III* (2006)
*Star Trek* (2009)
*Super 8* (2011)
*Star Trek Into Darkness* (2013)
*Star War: Episode VII – The Force Awakens* (2015)

**As producer:**
*The Pallbearer* (1996)
*The Suburbans* (1999)
*Joy Ride* (2001)
*Mission: Impossible III* (2006)
*Cloverfield* (2008)
*Star Trek* (2009)
*Morning Glory* (2010)

*Mission: Impossible – Ghost Protocol* (2011)
*Star Trek Into Darkness* (2013)
*Star Wars: Episode VII – The Force Awakens* (2015)

**As writer:**
*Taking Care of Business* (1990)
*Regarding Henry* (1991)
*Forever Young* (1992)
*Gone Fishin'* (1997)
*Armageddon* (1998)
*Mission: Impossible III* (2006)
*Super 8* (2011)
*Star Wars: Episode VII – The Force Awakens* (2015)

**As actor:**
*Regarding Henry* (1991)
*Six Degrees of Separation* (1993)

**TV**

**As co-creator and/or executive producer:**
*Felicity* (1998–2002) (Co-creator/executive producer)
*Alias* (2001–2006) (Creator/executive producer)
*Lost* (2004–2010) (Co-creator/executive producer)
*The Catch* (2005) (Creator/executive producer) *(Unaired)*
*What About Brian* (2006–2007) (Executive producer)
*Six Degrees* (2006–2007) (Executive producer)
*Fringe* (2008–2013) (Co-creator/executive producer)
*Anatomy of Hope* (2009) (Executive producer)
*Undercovers* (2010) (Co-creator/executive producer)

*Person of Interest* (2011–) (Executive producer)
*Alcatraz* (2012) (Executive producer)
*Shelter* (2012) (Executive producer)
*Revolution* (2012–2014) (Executive producer)
*Almost Human* (2013–2014) (Executive producer)
*Believe* (2014) (Executive producer)

**As guest director and/or guest star:**
*Jimmy Kimmel Live!* (2006) (Guest director)
*The Office* (2007) (Guest director)
*Family Guy* (2012) (Guest star)

## FICTION

*S.* with Doug Dorst (2013)

# SOURCES

The following print and online media outlets were invaluable during the researching and writing of this biography. Thank you to every publication.

**PRINT**

*Associated Press*
*Chicago Tribune*
*Daily Mail*
*The Daily Telegraph*
*Empire*
*Geek Monthly Magazine*
*The Guardian*
*The Hollywood Reporter*
*LA Times*
*Little White Lies*
*Metro*
*New York Daily News*
*New York Post*

*The New York Times*
*The New Yorker*
*The Observer*
*The Philadelphia Inquirer*
*Radio Times*
*Rolling Stone*
*SFX*
*The Times*
*USA Today*

**ONLINE**

http://blogs.indiewire.com
http://buzzymag.com
http://chicago.gopride.com
http://damngoodcup.com
http://edition.cnn.com
http://entertainment.time.com/2011
http://episode7news.com
http://geeknation.com
http://gointothestory.blcklst.com
http://herocomplex.latimes.com
http://idolmag.co.uk
http://insidetv.ew.com
http://io9.com
http://filmmakermagazine.com
http://filmschoolrejects.com
http://laist.com
http://lareviewofbooks.org
http://movies.about.com
http://movieline.com

http://news.moviefone.com
http://thequietus.com
http://screenrant.com
http://seriable.com
http://social.entertainment.msn.com
http://spinoff.comicbookresources.com
http://techland.time.com
http://trekmovie.com
http://uk.ign.com
http://usatoday30.usatoday.com
http://www.aintitcool.com
http://www.assignmentx.com
http://www.avclub.com
http://www.bbc.co.uk
http://www.bringmethenews.com
http://www.buddytv.com
http://www.craveonline.com
http://www.denofgeek.com
http://www.digitalspy.co.uk
http://www.ew.com
http://www.empireonline.com
http://www.esquire.co.uk
http://www.thefutoncritic.com
http://www.gq-magazine.co.uk
http://www.theguardian.com
http://www.hitfix.com
http://www.huffingtonpost.com
http://www.iamrogue.com
http://www.independant.co.uk
http://www.indielondon.co.uk

http://www.itsartmag.com
http://www.latimes.com
http://www.movies.com
http://www.moviesonline.ca
http://www.mtv.com
https://www.nerdist.com
http://www.nola.com
http://www.npr.org
http://www.nytimes.com
http://www.out.com
http://www.rogerebert.com
http://www.ropeofsilicon.com
http://www.salon.com
http://www.saltypopcorn.com
http://www.sandiegoreader.com
http://www.thescifishow.com
http://www.sheknows.com
http://www.slantmagazine.com
http://www.slashfilm.com
http://www.startrek.com
http://www.timeout.jp
http://www.torontosun.com
http://www.totalfilm.com
http://www.tv.com
http://www.tvguide.com
http://www.webwombat.com.au
http://www.wired.co.uk
http://www.wired.com
http://www.thewrap.com
and *Geek's Guide to the Galaxy, Podcast*

# ACKNOWLEDGEMENTS

Thank you to the following writers, journalists and authors whose work was integral to researching and writing this biography: Abbie Bernstein, Sanjiv Bhattacharya, David Bianculli, Robert Bianco, Rhys Blakely, Matt Bochenski, Geoff Boucher, Scott Bowles, Mike Bracken, Dave Bradley, Peter Bradshaw, Brad Brevet, Simon Brew, Doug Brod, Adam Buckman, Vincent Canby, Rob Carnevale, Debbie Chang, Adam Chitwood, Andrew Collins, Richard Corliss, Roth Cornet, Jonathan Crocker, Manohla Dargis, Sarah Dobbs, Christian DuChateau, Roger Ebert, Doug Elfman, Angie Errigo, David Fear, Dan Fienberg, Jack Foley, Ian Freer, Philip French, Jessica Furseth, Lawrence Van Gelder, Brian C. Gibson, Ryan Gilbey, Todd Gilchrist, Owen Gleiberman, Will Gompertz, Ed Gonzalez, Jamie Graham, Drew Grant, Michele Greppi, Lev Grossman, Mike Hale, Horatia Harrod, Carla Hay, Lauren Herstik, Jessie Heyman, James Hibberd, Logan Hill, John Hiscock, Josh Horowitz, Caryn James, Jeff Jensen,

Jo'C, Stuart Kelly, Bill Keveney, Shana Naomi Krochmal, Tim Lammers, Tom Lamont, Anthony Lane, Jill Lawless, John Scott Lewinski, Dave Lewis, Matthew Leyland, Matthew Lickona, Todd Longwell, Germain Lussier, Dani Lyman, Tim Martin, Craig McClean, Stuart McGurk, Gina McIntyre, Barry McIlheney, Graeme McMillan, Mary McNamara, Scott Mendelson, Julie Miller, Clint Morris, Noel Murray, Rebecca Murray, Scott Myers, Ian Nathan, Jerry Nunn, Jimmy O., Anthony Pascale, Ben Pearson, Jami Philbrick, James Poniewozik, Katie Puckrik, Andrew Pulver, Anthony Quinn, Christina Radish, Arun Rath, Simon Reynolds, Aaron Riccio, Olly Richards, Sheila Roberts, Tim Robey, Tasha Robinson, James Rocchi, Lacey Rose, Steve Rose, Joshua Rothman, Matt Roush, Maureen Ryan, Mike Ryan, Sukhdev Sandhu, Richard Z. Santos, Luke Savage, Sandy Schaefer, Peter Sciretta, A.O. Scott, Alan Sepinwall, Adam Sherwin, Jim Slotek, Tavis Smiley, Sid Smith, Alessandra Stanley, Linda Stasi, Jonathan Storm, Brian Ford Sullivan, Drew Taylor, Chris Tookey, Micah Towery, Peter Travers, Ken Tucker, Todd VanDerWerff, Jim Vejvoda, Alice Vincent, Richard Vine, Steve 'Frosty' Weintraub, Andrew Williams and Julie Wolfson.

Thank you also to Chris Mitchell and the staff at John Blake Publishing.

Apologies if I have missed out any names; if I have unintentionally overlooked you, please contact the publisher and the oversight will be corrected on reprint.

Visit my website www.neildanielsbooks.com.